FAMOUS REFORMERS

ZURICH
The Two-Towered Church is the Cathedral in which Zwingli Preached

FAMOUS REFORMERS

OF THE

Reformed and Presbyterian Churches

A MISSION STUDY MANUAL ON THE REFORMATION

BY

REV. PROF. JAMES I. GOOD, D. D., LL. D.

Professor of Reformed Church History in
Central Theological Seminary

Author of "Famous Women of the Reformed Church," "Famous Missionaries of the Reformed Churches," "Famous Places of the Reformed Churches," "Origin and History of the Reformed Church of Germany," "History of the Reformed Church in the United States," "History of the Reformed Church of Switzerland since the Reformation," "Historical Handbook of the Reformed Church," etc.

SOLID GROUND CHRISTIAN BOOKS
BIRMINGHAM, ALABAMA USA

Solid Ground Christian Books
PO Box 660132
Vestavia Hills AL 35266
205-443-0311
sgcb@charter.net
solid-ground-books.com

Famous Reformers of the Reformed and Presbyterian Churches
by James I. Good (1850-1924)

First published in 1916 by The Heidelberg Press
First Solid Ground edition October 2009

Cover image is Ulrich Zwingli.
Cover design by Borgo Design, Tuscaloosa, AL

ISBN: 978-159925-226-1

CONTENTS

	PAGE
FORE-WORD	vii
PREFACE	ix
CHAPTER 1—Zwingli and Luther	1
CHAPTER II—Zwingli and his Co-laborers, Juda, Ecolampadius and Vadian	21
CHAPTER III—The Completion of the Reformation in German Switzerland by Haller and Bullinger, and its Beginning in French Switzerland by Farel	41
CHAPTER IV—The Life and Work of John Calvin	61
CHAPTER V—The Completion of the Reformation in French Switzerland by Viret and Beza, and the Reformation in Holland	82
CHAPTER VI—The Reformed Reformers of Germany, Bucer and the Heidelberg Catechism	101
CHAPTER VII—The Reformers of Poland, Hungary, Italy and the Jews	121
CHAPTER VIII—The Reformers of Scotland, Hamilton, Wishart and Knox	141

ILLUSTRATIONS

	PAGE
THE CITY OF ZURICH	Frontispiece
ULRIC ZWINGLI	1
THE CONFERENCE AT MARBURG	21
THE CITY OF GENEVA	41
FAREL'S CALL TO CALVIN	61
THE ESCALADE AT GENEVA	82
THE CITY OF HEIDELBERG	101
THE TOMB OF WILLIAM OF ORANGE AT DELFT	121
KNOX AND QUEEN MARY	141

FOREWORD

One of the promising tendencies in the sphere of present-day religious life, especially among the young people, is the growing interest in the study of the history of the Christian Church. "Bible and Mission Study Classes"—the combination of terms is itself highly significant—are being successfully organized and maintained by so many agencies directly and indirectly connected with the Church, that we may fairly cherish the hope that, not only among youthful converts, but also among older members in our households of faith, the zeal that is so marked and so admirable a feature of our religious activities may be increasingly tempered with that knowledge which is ever the prime requisite for the cultivation of the noblest types of character and the promotion of the best forms of service.

And if truth is never more potent than when it is seen incarnated in human life, surely the study of the great Reformers of the sixteenth century—the leaders in that wondrous anabasis that brought the Church out of her medieval tutelage into the spacious liberties of the modern era—will ever be an effective means for the deepening and enriching of our conception of what Christianity is and what it may become.

I therefore heartily welcome this "Mission Study Manual on the Reformation." The author's many publications in this particular field and his long experience as a professor of history in a theological seminary are a sufficient guarantee for the general excellence of his work. He has succeeded in sketching the careers and achievements of the Reformers with admirable simplicity, clearness and conciseness, and in maintaining a due proportion among the varied elements of the outline as a whole. The style is frequently brightened with picturesque and dramatic touches and with references to historic landmarks and memorials that reveal the sympathetic interest of the narrator as an eyewitness. After the approved fashion in works of this sort, each chapter is followed by a series of questions designed to bring out the salient features of the text for the purpose of a class review. As explained in the Preface, the book is adjusted to the specific purpose of stimulating popular interest in the study of the Reformation considered primarily, though not exclusively, as an evangelistic and missionary enterprise.

We congratulate the author on the completion of this Manual on the eve of the four hundredth anniversary of the beginning of the Reformation, and express the hope that the book may be widely useful in spreading the knowledge of the Church of that period, and by this means furthering the kingdom of our Lord and Savior in our own day.

FREDERICK W. LOETSCHER.

Princeton Theological Seminary,
May 15, 1916.

PREFACE

The Reformation is a fitting study for its 400th anniversary (1917). We have endeavored in this Mission Study Manual to gather together, in as brief and popular a way as possible, the leading facts about the Reformers, especially of the Reformed Churches. As this is to be a Missionary Manual, we have, of course, emphasized the missionary spirit of the Reformers, an aspect which has been generally forgotten.

The Reformation and missions, what have they to do with each other? This,—that the Reformation was a great missionary movement, one of the greatest the Christian Church has ever seen; and it was both home and foreign missions. The Reformation has been studied from many standpoints, as a political movement, or as a polemical or a theological one, or as economic or moral or ecclesiastical. But to its missionary aspect little attention has been paid. Why should this be. It has been looked upon as mainly the arena of great doctrinal controversies or ecclesiastical strife, and its soul-saving feature has been forgotten? We fear that its polemics have caused some in this peace-loving age to turn away from it. They will recover their interest when its practical evangelistic spirit is fully brought out as in this book. The Reformation was a great missionary movement as much as any that we call missionary or evangelistic to-day.

We in this distant age, so long after the Reformation, are apt to consider it a sort of ready-made thing and to forget that it required a tremendous amount of hand-to-hand, personal work to make it a success. Andrew first found Peter, and John, James; these apostolic examples were followed in the Reformation. For, although the Reformation was largely a social movement that brought certain individuals to the front, as Luther and Zwingli; yet, after all, the personal element must not be forgotten, for it bulked largely in the success of the movement. And this personal effort was missionary effort. We are apt to forget that the Reformation was real missionary work—a calling of souls out of the darkness produced by the superstitions of Rome into the light of the Gospel of grace through Christ. And we forget that it began first with one man or a few men, who gathered others around them and thus the Reformation spread in ever-widening circles. The cause of its spread was missionary,—a zeal for souls,—a desire to tell them the new joy found in Protestantism. The Reformation was just as much missionary as our sending missionaries to Catholic lands, as Spain and Mexico and South America, to-day. We name the latter "missionaries." And there has just been held a great missionary convention at Panama to consider their work, for Latin-America is very much in the condition of Europe at the Reformation. And if these who go to Latin-America to-day are called "missionaries," then the Reformers and their co-workers should be called so, too, for they did the same kind of work among the same kind of people.

The Reformers talked to those around them about their new Gospel. They wrote many, many letters—a tremendous correspondence to persons and places, trying to lead them to the Evangelical faith. Church historians have made much of the doctrinal treatises of the Reformers and forgotten their correspondence, which is full of evangelism. Never since the days of the Apostle Paul and his Epistles was there so much consecrated letter-writing as in the Reformation; and much of it was missionary, for its aim was the spread of the Reformation by the conversion of individuals, cities or countries. The Reformers labored in their home towns and districts, and so were home mis-

PREFACE xi

sionaries; they also sent missionaries out into districts as yet unevangelized, and so they were foreign missionaries. This was more true of the Reformed than of the Lutheran, as the Reformed spread more widely. The Lutherans had this missionary spirit, and spread their gospel from Germany to Scandinavian lands; but the Reformed spread their gospel over all Europe except Scandinavia. But for their missonary and evangelistic zeal, we would not have our Church to-day.

Perhaps, to further elucidate this point, we may call attention to the fact that there have been and are three definitions of missions.

1. Only those are missions that are sent to non-Christian peoples. But this view has been given up by most Protestants as too narrow.

2. Missions include also the efforts to evangelize Christians who are not Protestant, as the Roman Catholics, Copts, etc. This view has been generally accepted.

3. Missions also include evangelization. This is the later view, and tends to make missions and evangelization run into each other. Thus revival services in our Churches are often called "missions." Evangelistic movements in our Christian lands are named "missions." It is this evangelistic aspect of the Reformation that becomes prominent in this book, although we believe that its definition of missions would be the second, for its work was the conversion of Roman Catholics to the Evangelical Gospel.*

We have endeavored in this book to prevent monotony and stimulate interest by calling attention to some special peculiarity in the life of each Reformer. Of course, in so brief a treatise much is omitted. And we especially regret that, on account of lack of space, some of the Reformers, as Lambert of Avignon, Blaurer of Constance, and Capito of Strasburg, have to be omitted. But, because we have thus

* It is to be remembered that this book is written for the Home Mission Board as well as for the Foreign Board.

limited the number of Reformers, we believe that their story will come out more vividly. And, though we have thus abbreviated the history, we believe that the great body of the most important facts of the Reformation is given, and given in their latest light. The colors in which this book is bound are historically significant. The colors of Zwingli were black and old gold. The cloth edition is bound in these colors. The paper edition is bound in black and gold. The nearest to the Zwingli colors that could be gotten, owing to the difficulties caused by the European war.

A cheap library of popular biographies has been prepared that ought to be used by the class in this study, and when the class is through with them, they can be put into the Sunday School library. They are Blackburn's "Ulric Zwingli," Blackburn's "William Farel," Vollmer's "John Calvin," Good's "The Heidelberg Catechism in Its Newest Light," and McCrie's "John Knox." They can be purchased for $2.85 a set.* The Presbyterians may not want the work on the "Heidelberg Catechism," and the Reformed may not want the "Life of Knox," and they can be deducted. But, as the set is so cheap, the whole set ought to be bought for use by the class and then placed in the Sunday School library. The most important works for the teacher are those of the "Heroes of the Reformation" series, as Jackson's "Zwingli," Walker's "Calvin," Baird's "Beza," and Cowan's "Knox." In the study of this Manual, the Presbyterians may leave out the part on the Heidelberg catechism, and the Reformed may omit the last chapter on Scotland, though we believe that in doing so, each will lose more than they think. A small leaflet will accompany this book, intended for the use of its teachers in Mission Study Classes, suggesting books and helps for preparation in teaching.* The author would also suggest to teachers of this book that questions of doctrines should be entirely

---

* The books and leaflet can be gotten from the Reformed Publication Board, 15th and Race Streets, Philadelphia, Pa.

PREFACE xiii

subordinated to those of missions and evangelism. For this is a mission study book and missions should come to the fore.

The author desires to express his gratefulness to Rev. Prof. Frederick W. Loetscher, D.D., Rev. C. E. Schaeffer, D.D., Rev. W. E. Lampe, Rev. J. G. Rupp and to Mr. John H. Poorman for suggestions made on the manuscript of the book.

He would also add that this volume forms another of a set of works that he has for a number of years been writing, as "Famous Women of the Reformed Church," "Famous Missionaries of the Reformed Churches," and "Famous Places of the Reformed Churches." This "Famous Reformers of the Reformed Churches" adds to that set its fourth volume. We hope at some time to complete the set by a last volume on "Famous Men of the Reformed Churches." We now leave this volume to its readers, hoping that the reading and study of it will be both educational and inspirational—especially inspirational for missionary work; and that the Lord may use it in the furtherance of His kingdom on earth.

ULRICH ZWINGLI

FAMOUS REFORMERS

CHAPTER I

THE FIRST REFORMERS—ZWINGLI AND LUTHER

I. *The Reformation and Missions.*

The Reformation, that great movement of the sixteenth century, out of which Protestantism was born, can be viewed from different standpoints. It has been looked at in Church History largely as a polemical movement—as a tremendous controversy in doctrine and religious life between Roman Catholicism and Protestantism. But, as this is a missionary study-book, we will look upon it as an evangelistic and missionary movement, and this will give a new perspective to it.* For evangelization played a prominent part in the work of the Reformers. They did personal hand-to-hand work; and they also either went themselves or sent missionaries into regions as yet unevangelized by Protestantism.

It will be an interesting study, we hope, to watch the birth and growth of the missionary spirit in the Reformers and to see how they struck the keynote for all the future Protestants. The Reformation was a great missionary revival. Would that the Protestant Church since the Reformation had had the missionary zeal the Reformers had! Our great modern missionary movements are only a return to that of the Reformation. That founded the Protestant Church; this converts a world. The Reformation is there-

---

* For a defence of this aspect, see the preface.

fore a very suitable mission study for 1917, its 400th anniversary.

II. *Preparation for the Reformation.*

The preparation for the Reformation was of two kinds, a secular and a religious one.

1. Viewed secularly, there were five events that led the way to it. Three of them were mechanical inventions: printing, the compass and gunpowder. One was geographical: the discovery of America in 1492. And the fifth was historical: the capture of Constantinople by the Turks in the fifteenth century, which forced eastern scholars westward, and so led to humanism, or the revival of classic education.

2. The religious preparation lay in three "Reformers before the Reformation": Wickliffe, Huss and Savonarola. Wickliffe was an Englishman, and was the most Protestant of them all, holding to the supremacy of Scripture and denying transubstantiation. Huss was a Bohemian, and held to the supremacy of Scripture, but still held to transubstantiation. Savonarola was an Italian, and was a full Catholic in doctrine, but prepared for the Reformation by his denunciations of the evils of the papacy. The last two were martyred. Luther was somewhat influenced by Huss, and Zwingli, perhaps, by Savonarola through Picus de Mirandola.

III. *Birth and Education.*

Ulrich Zwingli, the founder of the Reformed Churches, was born in northeastern Switzerland, at the village of Wildhaus, in the canton of St. Gall, which is located in a high valley about 4,000 feet above sea-level. The low Swiss chalet, in which he was born, January 1, 1484, is there to-day, black with age. Zwingli's father, the magistrate of the district, saw he was too bright to be a shepherd boy, and at the age of eight sent him away to school. His education was guided by his uncle, his father's brother, who was priest at Wesen, about fifteen miles south of Wildhaus. There was a providence in this, for his uncle was inclined to the new learning of that day, called humanism. Its more liberal spirit reacted against the narrow scholasticism of the Catholic Church and thus prepared the way for the Reformation. It was the liberalizing influence of this uncle that prepared Zwingli to later become the Reformer.

After studying in his uncle's school for two years, he was sent to school to Little Basle (opposite Basle, on the east side of the Rhine), where he began to reveal remarkable ability in his studies, especially in debate and music. About three years later he was sent to the school at Bern, which was noted for its humanism, and he remained there until sixteen years of age. His stay there was cut short by this incident. He later became the most musical of all the Reformers, playing seven instruments. The Dominican monks at Bern, seeing his ability and remarkable love for music, tried to get him to join their Order. Had he done so, he would have become a monk-reformer, as was Luther. But providence wanted the Reformation in Switzerland to be different from that of Luther,—to be begun by a priest-reformer, and by one who was, especially, a scholar in the new learning, humanism. Zwingli had gone so far toward joining the Dominicans as to live in their monastery. But then came the command of his father, perhaps at the instigation of his liberal-minded uncle, calling him home, so that he might be saved from monkhood. He was then sent to the university of Vienna, where he remained for two years, giving attention especially to philosophical studies, though there were humanistic influences there.

IV. *The Crisis in His Education.*

Zwingli progressed rapidly in his education. In 1502 he returned to Basle to teach, and also to study in the university. Here, fortunately, he attended the lectures of a Professor Thomas Wyttenbach. Wyttenbach had been born at Biel, a town west of Bern, and, after lecturing at Basle to Zwingli, he some years later went back to his birthplace to become its Protestant Reformer. Just as Ananias, who brought Paul out of the darkness of soul at Damascus, is forgotten in the greater glory of his convert, so Wyttenbach is forgotten in the greater glory of his pupil, Zwingli. Zwingli always spoke of him as "the most learned and holiest of men," and in his letters calls him "his dear preceptor." This reveals the debt that he felt he owed to his teacher.

Wyttenbach planted in his mind three seed-thoughts, that afterward came to harvest and produced the Reformation. Luther became a Reformer by emphasizing the doctrine of justification by faith, but Zwingli approached the Reformation from a somewhat different viewpoint, namely (and these were the three seed-thoughts that Wyttenbach taught him):

1. The supreme authority of Scripture,—the Bible was to be the guide rather than the Church, as the Catholics held.
2. Sins are forgiven through the death of Christ, and not through the Virgin Mary, as Catholics held.
3. The sale of indulgences was a fraud and a cheat.

Zwingli was under Wyttenbach but a few months, but in that short time Wyttenbach left an indelible impression upon him. These three seed-thoughts slumbered in his mind for about ten years, and then, as we shall see, they came to harvest as he began the Reformation at Einsedeln. How wonderful and eternally-lasting is the influence of a Christian teacher. All the Reformed and Presbyterian Churches, now numbering about thirty millions of adherents, have come directly out of this Reformed Reformation, and are the result of these three seed-thoughts of Wyttenbach. Indeed, all the other Protestant Churches, except the Lutheran, have indirectly come out of it, so that Wyttenbach's influence through Zwingli is affecting more than one hundred millions who are living to-day. What an inspiration, this, to the Christian worker! It is one of the most remarkable illustrations in all Church history.

We now come to the study of Zwingli's conversion. The study of a man's conversion, especially of a great man like Zwingli, is a very interesting subject, and we may well pause to follow its steps carefully.

V. *Zwingli's First Charge—Glarus (1506-1516).*

In 1506 Zwingli was called as priest by the congregation at Glarus, situated about fifty miles southeast of Zurich. He remained there for ten years. The church in which he preached was burned down by a conflagration in 1861, which destroyed most of the town. And the new church is a simultaneous church,—that is, one in which both Catholics and Reformed worship, though at different hours. The communion cup used by Zwingli is still there.

The most interesting question about this period is whether there are any signs of his becoming a Reformer. It is very evident that as yet he was only a humanist; and yet in his case, as in that of a number of others, humanism was the bridge over which he passed to Protestantism. He revealed his love of humanism during this period in several ways:

1. He began the study of the Greek language about 1513. The Latin language was the sacred language to the Catholics, so the study of the Greek prepared him to become a Reformer when he later gained possession of the Greek New Testament.

2. He started a school which was attended by young men of the best families and in which he taught the new humanistic methods of education. Some of his students, who afterward became prominent, as Tschudi, bore witness to his wonderful power as a teacher.

3. He came into correspondence with Erasmus, the leader of the humanists.

But the Protestant was beginning to appear in the midst of the humanist, though still faintly. There are several signs that prophesied the coming Reformer. These were:

1. A *linguistic* preparation (the knowledge of the Greek), which prepared him to later read the New Testament and thus see the difference between it and the Romish Church.

2. A *political* preparation. He paid three visits to Italy as chaplain to the Swiss troops hired by foreign powers. These visits to Italy opened his eyes to the great wickedness of the papacy, for the proverb then was "the nearer Rome, the worse Christian."

3. A *liturgical* preparation. While in Italy, he found at Milan that the old liturgy of Ambrose, the early Church Father, differed from the Romish liturgy of his day. A second discovery that he made was at Mollis, a village just north of Glarus, of a liturgy of two hundred years before his time, which said that at communion the cup was given to the laity, whereas the Catholics in his day gave only the bread to them.

4. A *doctrinal* preparation. He began to doubt the doctrine of the intercession of the saints, one of the fundamental doctrines of Romanism.*

VI. *His Second Charge at Einsedeln (1516-1518).*

In 1516 he left Glarus for Einsedeln. The cause of his departure was the opposition of a minority in his congregation because he was so outspoken against the foreign military service of the Swiss. We thus see that he was a political reformer even before he became a religious one. Einsedeln was a very different field from Glarus. It was a pilgrimage-place in an upper valley four thousand feet above sea-level, and about twenty-five miles northeast of Zurich. Here Zwingli was not priest, as there was no parish. But he was preacher for the pilgrims who came from Switzerland and southern Germany. The name Einsedeln means hermit, and hither Meinrad, the hermit, had come in the ninth century and founded a monastery.

*Egli, *Schweizerische Reformations-Geschichte*, page 35.

ZWINGLI AT EINSEDELN

It had in it one of the most sacred of the Romish relics, the image of the Black Virgin, which was believed to have power to forgive sins. There was a providence in his appointment to this place, for, as he had no pastoral duties, it gave him ample time for study. Like Paul in Arabia, and Luther at the Wartburg, he was set aside in quietness so as to be prepared for his great work as Reformer. It was here that he began preaching the Gospel of Protestantism, for he said, "I began to preach the gospel of Christ in 1516, before any one in my locality had as much as heard of Luther."

The event that made Zwingli do this was the publication of a book. Oh, how great is the power of a book, especially when that book is the Bible. In 1516 Erasmus published the Greek New Testament. As Zwingli read it, a flood of light burst on his mind, as he saw how different the Romish Church was from the New Testament. He copied in his own handwriting all the Epistles of Paul in Greek,* and committed whole Epistles to memory. This later proved of great value to him in his disputations with the Catholics. In thus committing Scripture, he is an example to be imitated by Christians to-day.

And now the seed-thoughts planted in his mind by Wyttenbach sprang forth to harvest, and he began the Reformation. His progress seems to have been gradual, but at that time he seems to have been farther advanced than Luther when the latter nailed the theses on the church door at Wittenberg, October 31, 1517. For he was already emphasizing the central doctrine of Protestantism, that sins were forgiven through the ransom of Christ.** Zwingli had gone deeper than Luther, for he believed in the ransom of Christ, which is the root and basis of justification. He was, too, a hero of great moral courage in

---

* The manuscript of this is in the Zwingli museum at Zurich.

** Bullinger, History of the Reformation, page 9.

preaching this doctrine, for over the door of his abbey were the words, "Here sins are forgiven by the Virgin Mary," and within was the Black Virgin worshiped by the pilgrims. And yet he boldly preached that sins were forgiven by Christ, not by Mary. His preaching was revolutionary, for some of the pilgrims carried away these new doctrines with them. Thus they were scattered far and wide, and he gained great fame for his boldness and eloquence.

VII. *Zwingli's First Year at Zurich—1519.*

Zwingli's fame as a preacher became so great that the little mountain abbey could not hold him. In the latter part of 1518 he was called to be the head priest at the cathedral of Zurich. He went to Zurich as a missionary to tell them the new Gospel he had learned from the Word of God and to preach to them about the ransom of Christ, for they were in the darkness of Romanism. Zurich was at that time a walled city of perhaps 10,000 inhabitants, the chief city in northeastern Switzerland. Here on New Year's Day, 1519, he startled his congregation by announcing that he would preach to them on the Gospel of Matthew, verse by verse. In doing this he was making prominent one of his cardinal principles, namely, the supremacy of Scripture. But this was a very different kind of preaching from that to which they had been accustomed, which consisted of saint stories, etc. It created great excitement, but many found in it the spiritual food for which they had long been yearning. He also showed his missionary spirit by trying to convert the country people as well as the city folk, for he began preaching on Fridays as well as on Sundays, as Friday was market day and that brought the people of the canton to Zurich. The result was this new Gospel was spread through all the canton of Zurich as well as the city. Soon after he came to Zurich, Samson came there selling indulgences, but Zwingli preached so hard against him that Samson left not only Zurich, but

Switzerland. But the labors of the young priest proved greater than his strength. He, in order to recuperate, went to a neighboring watering place, Ragatz-Pfaffers, about seventy miles southeast of Zurich, where in a picturesque narrow gorge were healing springs. Then the plague broke out in Zurich, and, like a faithful pastor, he came back to Zurich to minister to his flock. He soon fell a victim to the plague, and was so sick that it was reported that he was dead. But God preserved him for great purposes. However, this severe illness greatly deepened his religious experience. This is shown by the hymn that he composed during this sickness, which consisted of three beautiful short prayers in verse.*
He was now, both by study and religious experience, prepared for the great work that was about to come upon him, namely, the Reformation of the city of Zurich.

VIII. *The Beginning of the Reformation at Zurich— 1520-1523.*

Zwingli's preaching soon began to exert great influence in Zurich. Already at the beginning of 1520 he had over 2,000 adherents. In 1520 the city council ordered that all preaching must be according to the Word of God. In 1522 matters began to come to a crisis. As a result of Zwingli's preaching, Christopher Froschouer, the great printer of Zurich, refused to fast in Lent. Zwingli defended this position about fasts. The Bishop of Constance, in whose diocese Zurich was, complained to the councils of Zurich against Zwingli. The Reformation was in great danger. Zwingli betook himself to prayer, and, lo, on April 9 the great council of the city decided against the bishop. Then the bishop had a decree passed at the Swiss Diet against Zurich. But Zurich went on, nevertheless, in her reforms. On July 17 Zwingli did what may be called personal missionary work for the conversion of Lambert of Avignon. Lambert was a Franciscan monk, with whom Zwingli de-

* See Jackson's Life of Zwingli, 132-134.

bated publicly about the intercession of the saints, and so powerfully that Lambert was converted to Protestantism. On November 11, 1522, the Zurich council took an action that virtually was the beginning of a declaration of independence from the power of the Bishop of Constance, and so from the Catholic Church. It was when Zwingli brought matters to an issue by resigning, because certain of his duties were against his Protestant views. The council accepted his resignation, but, *without asking permission of the bishop*, requested him to continue to preach. It also went farther and forbade the foreign service of the Swiss, and also refused to give up to the bishop the Evangelical pastors at Zurich.

It was very evident that matters were approaching a crisis. This crisis came in 1523. On January 29 there was a great disputation held at Zurich. Zwingli had, ten days before, just as Luther had done at Wittenberg in 1517, nailed up 67 theses for debate. These were much more Protestant than Luther's were, though it is to be remembered that Luther's were five years earlier. Zwingli defended his theses out of the Bible, and gained a great victory, as the council ordered that nothing be preached but what was founded on the Word of God. A second great conference was held on October 26, 1523, before a large audience. A voice or two were feebly lifted up to defend Catholicism, but Zwingli and Leo Juda literally annihilated their opponents out of the Bible as they discussed images and the mass. As a result of this conference, Zurich committed herself more fully than ever to Protestantism.

Zwingli, in November, 1523, preached against images. Thomas Platter tells the story that he was at that time sexton in the Fraumünster Church, Zurich. One morning when Zwingli was to preach in the church, Platter found he had no wood for making a fire to heat the church. He looked into the church and saw no one there, so he took a wooden statue of John from the nearest altar, and as he threw it into the stove he said, "Little John, now stoop, for you must go into the stove." When it began to burn it produced a very ugly odor, due to the paint on it. So he closed the stove door. The schoolmaster, Myconius, came in and asked, "Have you had good wood?" and Platter thought that John had done his best. As the congregation began to sing the hymn, two of the priests, who had come in, began quarreling about the missing statue, the one calling the other a Lutheran and charging him with having stolen his John. These facts never were made public until many years later when Platter was at Basle. The next year (1524) the images were taken out of the churches, and in December of that year the monasteries were suppressed.

IX. *The Completion of the Reformation at Zurich—1525.*

By the end of 1524 the only remnant of Catholicism was the mass. Finally, in the spring of 1525, the Zurich council ordered that on Thursday of Passion Week, April 13, the Lord's Supper should be celebrated in the Protestant fashion, by using bread instead of wafers, and by giving the cup to the laity in addition to the bread. Thus, after six years of struggle, from 1519 to 1525, the Reformation was victorious. Zwingli was its leader, and he was aided by Leo Juda, who had become pastor of St. Peter's Church, Zurich, and by Myconius, the schoolmaster of the Fraumünster Church there.

On July 19, 1525, Zwingli began a new kind of service in the chapel of th cathedral, which was called a "prophesying." It was a sort of conference and prayer-meeting, the forerunner of modern prayer-meetings. In this he was later followed by Haller at Bern, Calvin at Geneva, and Lasco in London. Zwingli also, in 1525 wrote his most important work, "A Commentary on True and False Religion." It was a brief system of theology describing the different Protestant doctrines and refuting Catholicism. But all this victory was gained only after great effort and also great danger to Zwingli, for his life was often threatened.

The life of Zwingli, after he had by his missionary zeal evangelized Zurich, divided itself into two parts,—his relation to Luther and his relation to the other Swiss cantons, who by his leadership were led out of Catholicism to the light of the Gospel. We will now take up his relations to Luther.

X. *Luther's Youth and Education.*

Martin Luther was born at Eisleben, November 10, 1483, but his father soon moved to Mansfield, where Martin went to school. He later was educated at Magdeburg and then at Eisenach. There, as a boy, he was accustomed to sing carols in the streets and thus gain money for his education. His fine voice attracted the notice of Ursula Cotta, who belonged to one of the leading families at Eisenach, and she welcomed him to her table. At Eisenach he also had as his teacher Trebonius, who would always on entering the school, take off his cap to the boys, because he said he did not know but some of them might become famous,—a prophecy afterwards fulfilled in Luther. Luther went (1501) to the university of Erfurt. He was a serious-minded youth, and later had for his motto: "To pray well is half the study."

In 1505 he entered the Augustinian monastery at Erfurt. He was brought to this decision when caught in a terrible thunder storm. Then, at a fearful flash of lightning, he threw himself to the earth and made a vow that he would become a monk. Two years later he was ordained to the priesthood. In 1508 he was made professor of theology at the university of Wittenberg. Two years later he was sent to Rome on business of his Order. When he came in sight of that city, so sacred to all Catholics, he threw himself on the ground and exclaimed, "Hail to thee, holy Rome." There he climbed the "Sacred Stairs" of Pilate's Judgment Hall, and when doing so the words "the just shall live by faith" came to him.

XI. *Luther's Conversion.*

The conversion of Luther, like that of Zwingli, is a

profoundly interesting subject. Formerly Luther's conversion was described as sudden and emotional. Later biographers make it more gradual. In the early days of his manhood he was very zealous in his fastings and self-mortification, hoping thereby to save his soul. But he was disappointed in them, for they gave him no peace. Then the kind advice of Staupitz, the vicar-general of his order, and the reading of the mystic theology of Tauler gave him some light. He was especially prepared for his conversion by a growing study of the Bible and of the works of Augustine, the early Church Father. The text "The just shall live by faith" led him to rely more on faith than on works for salvation. In his lectures on the Psalms (1513-15) and on Romans and Galatians (1515-17) he used the works of Lefevre, the Reformed Reformer of France, who, before either Luther or Zwingli, taught in 1512 the doctrine of justification by faith. Erasmus' New Testament of 1516 greatly influenced him, as it did Zwingli. He now inclined to the Bible rather than to the theology of Catholicism founded on Aristotelianism. In 1517 he seems to have held to salvation by faith and yet "could not discard his doubts about the certainty of salvation or his monkish aversion that it was against true humility to thus count on God's mercy."

Then occurred the event that produced the crisis. Tetzel, the Dominican monk, came to Germany to sell indulgences. An indulgence was a papal pardon that insured one of freedom from punishment without any repentance, provided money were paid. Luther protested against this by nailing up 95 theses on the church door of the Castle Church at Wittenberg, October 31, 1517.

"That," says one of Luther's biographers, "was the birthday of the Reformation." Hardly; for these theses were not at all Protestant. Another of his biographers, Koestlin, speaks of them as "the germ of the Reformation." That is truer. There is nothing said in them about justification by faith. Luther, in them, believes in Catholic indulgences, for he says there, "Cursed is he who speaks against the truth of apostolical pardons."

1. What he condemns are not indulgences, but their *abuse*. For the whole business of indulgences had become a great commercial monopoly by which the rich banking house of Fuggers at Augsburg and the Archbishop of Mayence made high commissions. As we would say now, "The trusts had gotten hold of the business."

2. Luther also protested in these theses against the *papal* indulgences, over against those given by the bishops and clergy, which he still endorsed.

3. That he was not yet a Protestant he himself later says, for he called himself at this time "a most insane papist," and said that he would have killed any one who denied obedience to the pope. He says (1520): "Some two years ago I wrote a little book on indulgences, which I now deeply regret having published, for at that time I held that indulgences should not be altogether rejected, seeing that they were approved by the common consent of men." That book, published a year later than his theses on indulgences, showed he still believed in them.

Now, if Luther had believed in salvation by faith, as Protestants do, he never would have there endorsed the Catholic view of indulgences, which has its basis in justification by works; for part of the Catholic doctrine of indulgence was the idea that the deeds or the money, prescribed by the priest in the indulgence, were of value to save. And yet, on the other hand, his belief in salvation by faith instead of by works was growing. How shall we harmonize it with his view of indulgences? Perhaps the explanation is that Luther was then like the great Church Father whom his Order revered, Augustine. Augustine held to the two opposing theories of Evangelicalism and Sacramentarianism. According to the former he held that men were saved by grace,—that is, by the election of God— God's act; according to the latter he held to regeneration by baptism,—that is, men were saved by man's act—the act of the priest. Like him, Luther seems here to have held to salvation by faith and also by works, as the Catholic Church later did at the Council of Trent. But, as the result showed, the former was growing more rapidly than the latter. It is evident, therefore, that when he nailed up the theses he was not yet a Protestant. Even after it, in 1519, says Doumergue, he held to purgatory, saint worship and transubstantiation, and did not renounce the elevation of the host until 1543. Luther's act in nailing up the "theses" was an epoch-making event, but he was not yet a Protestant. Zwingli much more quickly and fully renounced these Romish errors.

XII. *Beginnings of Luther's Reformation.*

But his "theses" struck a popular chord in Germany. They were the match that ignited the powder-magazine. Large parts of Germany had become hostile to papal indulgences and abuses. In two weeks the theses had spread all over Germany, and in a month all over Europe. The next year he went to Heidelberg for his Order, and there in his theses he comes out clearly on justification by faith. In the summer of 1519 he had a disputation at Leipsic with Eck, the great Catholic champion. Then he went a step farther and declared that the papacy rested not on divine authority, but was a human institution. By the end of that year he laid emphasis on the priesthood of all believers, over against the priesthood of the Romish Church.

But it was in the year 1520 that he made the formal declaration of his independence from Rome. In that year he published three works which formulated his new views. The first was his "Appeal to the German Nobility." This was a ringing trumpet note that woke up all Germany. Its theme was the responsibility and duty of the laity in church matters. It urged the secular power to take a hand in the regeneration of Germany and not leave it to the Church. This was followed by his "Babylonish Captivity," in which he attacked the Catholic doctrine of the sacraments and showed how they were perverted so as to corrupt the Christian life. A third book was his "Christian Liberty," on the liberty the Christian enjoys through the doctrine of justification by faith. These three treatises were the chief reforming works of Luther. The first showed the reformation of the state; the second, of the Church, and the third, of the inner Christian life. When the pope had published a bull against him, he burned it, December 10, 1520, at Wittenberg. This was a most heroic act.

XIII. *Worms and Wartburg.*

The year 1521 was also a fateful year for Luther. The pope finally, on January 3, 1521, pronounced the ban on him. It remained now to be seen whether it could be carried out in Germany. He was summoned to Worms in April, 1521. He was given a safe-conduct, but it was commonly expected that it would be violated as had been done to Huss a century before. But Luther defied the danger, and declared he would go to Worms "if there were as many devils as there were tiles on the roofs of the houses." At the diet he was asked whether he would recant what he had written. He refused to do so, closing his address with the famous words, "God help me. Amen." The diet then ordered the ban of the empire to be placed upon him. To save him from this, he was secretly kidnapped and hidden in the castle of the Wartburg near Eisenach. There he remained for about a year, hidden under the name of Squire George. He spent much of his time in translating the New Testament into German, which was published 1522. While he was absent from Wittenberg, matters there were getting into confusion. The mild Phillip Melancthon, who had been called as his associate in 1517, and who was a fine scholar and strong humanist, was unable to control the erratic Carlstadt, one of the preachers at Wittenberg. So Luther returned to Wittenberg in March, 1522, and restored order.

XIV. *Political Events Affecting the Reformation.*

The ban of the empire still hung over Luther. But there is an important providence to be noted in connection with the Reformation. Whenever Protestantism was greatly threatened by the Catholic powers, then the Turks would threaten to invade Germany; and the Emperor, for the sake of getting men and money to carry on war, instead of oppressing the Protestant princes, would have to conciliate them. Luther was also protected by his prince, the Elector of Saxony, who was supported by a constantly increasing number of Protestant princes. In 1523 the Peasants' War broke out. This was an economic uprising of the peasants against the princes and the authorities, as well as a religious revolt against Catholicism. It represented Protestant radicalism. Yet Luther took strong grounds against it and in favor of law and order. It was finally suppressed in 1525. But Carlstadt's extremes at Wittenberg in 1522 and the Peasants' War had an unfortunate effect on Luther. They made him become more conservative. Zwingli represented the progressive Reformation, Luther, the conservative. Luther now became more conservative, both in regard to doctrine, worship and church government. It was in connection with doctrine that he became involved in a controversy with the Reformed, especially on the Lord's Supper.

XV. *Luther's Controversy with the Reformed.*

Luther in 1526 began attacking Zwingli for his doctrine of the Lord's Supper. The difference between them was this: Both rejected the Catholic doctrine of transubstantiation—that is, that the bread and wine at the Supper were changed into the very body and blood of Christ. Zwingli (especially at first) went to the other extreme and held to the memorial view,—that the prime reference of the Lord's Supper was to the sacrifice of Christ on the cross, of which it was a memorial. This Luther attacked. For he held that the real body and blood of Christ were present with the elements. Luther attacked the Zwinglian view because it seemed to him to have *no* presence of Christ at the Supper. Zwingli, on the other hand, attacked the Lutheran doctrine, because it required a *material* presence of Christ's body with the elements of the Supper. In exegesis they differed as to the interpretation of the word "is" in the phrase "This is my body." Zwingli claimed that the word was used *figuratively*, and meant "signifies." Luther claimed that the word must be taken *literally*,—that it expressed a fact and not a figure. Such was the controversy that unhappily divided the Lutherans and Reformed at a time when they most needed to be united against Rome. Of the Conference at Marburg, where Luther and Zwingli met and debated the Lord's Supper, we will speak later. This controversy of Luther with Zwingli and the Reformed continued up to the time of the latter's death and later.

XVI. *Luther's Later Years.*

After the Peasants' War the Catholic powers of Germany still tried to suppress the Protestants. At the diet of Spires, in 1529, they decided to take violent measures against the Protestants. This led to the delivery of a protest to the Emperor, signed by five princes and fourteen free cities of the empire. Because of this act we are to-day called "Protestants." In 1530 the next diet was held at Augsburg. Luther dared not go to it, as he was under the ban of the empire, but stayed at Coburg. Melancthon attended it, and laid before the Emperor the Lutheran creed, the Augsburg Confession. Luther then returned to Wittenberg, where he spent the rest of his life in teaching in the university. He also labored to introduce Protestantism into new districts and to organize the Churches. He died on February 18, 1546.

Luther's life was the most dramatic of the four great Reformers. He stands out as a great heroic figure. His great work was as the founder of the Lutheran Church, which in the Reformation spread from Germany into Scandinavian lands. Next to that was his translation of the Bible into German, which was published in 1534.

QUESTIONS

ZWINGLI

What is the relation of the Reformation to Missions?
What events and what persons prepared the way for the Reformation?
When and where was Zwingli born?
Describe his education?
Describe Wyttenbach's influence over him?
Where was his first charge?
What signs of the coming Reformer appeared at Glarus?
What did Zwingli do at Einsedeln?
What beginnings of the Reformation were there at Einsedeln?
Describe his first preaching at Zurich?
Describe the various steps of the Reformation at Zurich
What completed the Reformation at Zurich?

LUTHER

When and where was Luther born?
Describe his education.
Describe his visit to Rome.
What influences prepared him to become a Reformer?
What were indulgences, and how did he attack them?
What two opposing views were struggling in Luther for the mastery?
What effect on Germany had his theses?
What three works did he publish in 1520?
What was the pope's bull, and what did Luther do with it?
Describe his attendance at the diet of Worms.
What did he do while at the Wartburg?
Why did he return to Wittenberg?
What was the difference between Zwingli and Luther on the Lord's Supper?

How long did the controversy continue?
Why are we called Protestants?
What occurred at the diet of Augsburg?
When did Luther die?
What was Luther's character and work?

THE CONFERENCE AT MARBURG
Zwingli and Luther are Standing to the Right, the Latter Pointing His Finger to the Table

CHAPTER II

Zwingli and His Fellow-Reformers

I. *The Spread of the Reformed Doctrine.*

The Reformed Church having been established at Zurich by 1525, entered on its next stage, namely, its spread to the other cantons. Here Zwingli appears as a true home missionary, as were indeed all the Reformers. The Reformation was a great missionary age. Everywhere and in all directions we see them striving to lead men to Christ. Zwingli did this to the other cantons in Switzerland, and even to regions beyond, as Germany. His zeal should be an inspiration for home missions to-day. Wherever he heard the Gospel was being favorably received, or that there was an opening for it, there he hastened to write a letter or to go himself. Thus in 1524, when he heard that the Toggenburg, the district where he was born, accepted the Gospel, he wrote to its council a letter congratulating them on it. In 1525 he wrote to the canton of the Grisons urging them to aid the spread of Protestantism and also help Zurich.

II. *The Conference at Baden.*

The first step that prepared for the reception of the Gospel elsewhere was the Conference at Baden, May 21, 1526, in which the Catholics planned to crush the Reformation at Zurich. Baden was not in the canton of Zurich, but was close enough to have great influence there, being about fifteen miles west of Zurich. Zwingli did not attend the Conference. As Baden was a very bigoted Catholic city, the city council of Zurich forbade his attendance, as he probably would have suffered violence. He, however, spent more time in outlining arguments for the speakers there than if he had been debating there. For messengers brought Zwingli the report of the Conference each evening. To these he replied during the night and his replies were sent to Baden by morning.

One of these messengers was Thomas Platter, who thus tells the story. It was arranged that a young man in the Conference should each day write down what was said, and that either Platter or another young man would carry it from Baden to Zwingli. When they were asked at the city gate of Baden what their business was, they replied that they brought chickens to Baden to sell, which was true. This interchange of messages continued until the last day of the disputation, when Platter carried the report to Zurich. But he started late and so came to Zwingli's house very late. He had to knock a long while before Zwingli's servant opened, who said, "Why so late? Can you not let Master Ulrich rest for one night? For six weeks he has not been in bed because of the disputation." Being admitted, Platter knocked a long while at Zwingli's door, until Zwingli woke up and received him, when he told him what had been done at Baden. In an hour or so, Zwingli's reply was on the way to Baden, taken by the other young man, as Platter was too tired to return. When this messenger came to the gate of Baden, it was yet dark. The gate was locked. He found a wagon of hay standing at the gate waiting for it to be opened. He climbed up in the hay-wagon and fell asleep. When he woke up, he found that the wagon had gone in through the gate, and had brought him to the market-place at Baden, right in front of the house where he was to deliver Zwingli's reply to Ecolampadius.

Although Zwingli was not at the Conference, yet fortunately the Reformed found a new champion in Ecolampadius, the Reformer at Basle. The champion of the Catholics was Eck, who came there from his victory over Luther at Leipsic, as he claimed. We shall later in connection with

BERN AND MARBURG CONFERENCES

the life of Ecolampadius describe this Conference. The Catholics claimed a victory there, but the facts are against it, for the Conference undoubtedly spread the Reformation, especially in the cantons of Bern and Basle.

III. *The Conference at Bern.*

The next great event was the Conference at Bern, January 6, 1528. This was a great missionary effort on the part of Zwingli and others to bring that largest of the Swiss cantons into the Reformed Church. Zwingli attended it as did the leading Reformers from other Protestant cantons. We shall not describe this Conference here, as it will come up again in the life of Haller, the Reformer at Bern. As we shall there see, Zwingli was easily the leader in the Conference and exerted a great influence. This Conference proved to be a great victory for the Reformed, because by it they gained the large canton of Bern. And it also opened up the way, as we shall see in the life of Farel, for the spread of Protestantism to the French cantons of southwestern Switzerland.

IV. *The Conference at Marburg.*

The next great event was the Conference at Marburg in 1529. We also see in this the missionary enterprise of Zwingli and the other Reformers. The doctrines of Zwingli had been spread over German Switzerland. Zwingli hoped they would now find an entrance into Germany, for the Conference of Marburg was the prophecy of the permanent founding of the Reformed Church in Germany, later at Heidelberg.

Landgrave Phillip of Hesse, one of the leading princes of Germany, was anxious to bring the Lutherans and the Reformed together. In order to do this, he arranged that a Conference should be held at Marburg in western Germany. Zwingli, fearing that the council of Zurich would not permit him to go on account of the danger, secretly left Zurich on September 3, 1529. He traveled by way of Basle. From Basle he went down the Rhine by boat to

Strassburg. Then under an armed guard, he went to the border of Hesse on the Rhine, crossing it at St. Goar, or Rheinfels. He arrived in Marburg on September 27th, accompanied by other Reformed Reformers, as Ecolampadius of Basle, and Bucer and Hedio of Strassburg. This Conference was the only time when all the Reformers came together. Luther and Melancthon were there, together with other Lutheran Reformers. It looked as if the two Churches, Lutheran and Reformed, might be united.

On October 1st, the public debate took place in the great hall of the castle, in the presence of Landgrave Phillip of Hesse and Duke Ulrich of Wurtemberg. These princes sat at one end of the table, while the leading Reformers sat or stood around the table. There is a tradition that Luther wrote on the table in chalk the words, "This is my body," so that he might not weaken from his position on the Lord's Supper. For two days they debated, especially on the Lord's Supper. Zwingli and Ecolampadius so pressed Luther by the exegesis of the Scripture texts and quotations from the Church Fathers that finally he could answer no more, but pulling the cloth, on which he had written the words "This is my body" from the table, he held it up before them as his vindication.

But a sickness broke out in the crowded town and broke up the Conference. Before they separated, the Landgrave had them draw up fifteen Articles of Faith. Both sides agreed on all the Articles except on that about the Lord's Supper. As it was evident that they could not reach an entire agreement, the Swiss asked that they be recognized by Luther as brethren. But Luther refused, saying, "You have a different spirit from ours." Zwingli held out his hand to Luther but was refused, and so the Conference broke up (October 5th), without uniting the two Churches. But it made a favorable impression for Zwinglianism on Germany. Thus Lambert of Avignon, the Reformer of Hesse, declared he had come to the Conference with his mind like a sheet of white paper, ready to receive impressions. After the Conference he favored Zwingli, but unfortunately died soon. It also made the Landgrave so favorable that he proposed to the German princes an alliance with the Swiss, but it was rejected by the Lutherans. However, the city of Strassburg entered into an alliance with Zurich.

V. *Zwingli's Later Years.*

For the diet of Augsburg in Germany (1530), where Melancthon presented the first Lutheran creed, the Augsburg Confession, to the Emperor of Germany, Zwingli prepared a Confession of his own, which he sent to the Emperor, who, however, paid no attention to it. But it is interesting to note that it differed from the Augsburg Confession on the doctrine of the Lord's Supper, and like all the Reformed creeds, made the Bible prominent.

The last years of Zwingli were taken up with political alliances and with the spread and conservation of Protestantism. He had been criticized for the former, but it is to be remembered that Zurich was at that time peculiarly situated by being isolated. In 1527 she was excluded from the Swiss diet by the Catholic contons, and only the next year did Bern, Basle, Schaffhausen and the other Protestant districts unite with her to form the Protestant diet. In this we must not judge Zwingli by our day or by our American views of the separation of Church and State. Certain it is, that had Zwingli's views been carried out and a political alliance of all Protestants formed, the Protestants would not have suffered such losses as they did, especially in the Thirty Years' War, for Rome would have been held in check.

But Zwingli was also very busy introducing and building up Protestantism in the Catholic cantons of St. Gall, Appenzell and Thurgau, northeast of Zurich, and of Schaffhausen to the north. His letters reveal his activity there. At the end of 1529 he went to Frauenfeld, the capital of Thurgau, and organized the Reformed congregations into a synod, composed of about five hundred ministers from the Rhine valley. The next year he again went there to synod meeting. The result of his influence and work was that all those districts are now largely Potestant.

VI. *His Death at Cappel.*

The year 1531 was the last year of his life. It brought with it the Second Cappel War. The First Cappel War broke out in 1529, between the canton of Zurich and the five mountain cantons south of her: Lucerne, Zug, Schwytz, Uri and Unterwalden. These remained intensely Catholic and opposed the Protestantism of Zurich. In this First Cappel War, the two armies met for battle, but just as they were about to fight, peace was made. This peace has come down to us in history as the "milk-soup peace"; because when it was made, the soldiers of the one side brought milk and of the other side, bread. They threw the bread into the soup and both ate out of the same dish, as the symbol of peace. It was in connection with this war that Zwingli wrote his most famous hymn, "Guide, O Lord Thy Chariot Now."

But the First Cappel War had settled nothing permanently. So the war broke out again in 1531. The Protestant cantons had decided to lay an embargo upon the five Catholic cantons on wheat, and other necessary articles, until these cantons would give up foreign pensions, etc. Bern especially urged this procedure, and then left Zurich in the lurch to suffer from it. Suddenly the five Catholic cantons rose in war and marched on October 9, 1531, against Zurich. Zurich hurriedly gathered her army together, but she was greatly unprepared. Zwingli bade good-bye to his wife and family and went out as chaplain with the army. On October 11, 1531, the two armies met on the battlefield of Cappel. The 8,000 Catholic troops soon defeated the 2,700 in the Zurich army, although the latter fought bravely. Zwingli was knocked down while ministering to a soldier. Lying under a pear tree he was dying of his wounds. The Catholic troops came up and, finding him dying, asked him if he wanted a priest. He shook his head, saying, "No." His last words were (and they ought to be classic to every member of the Reformed faith): "They may kill the body, but they cannot kill the soul." When his identity was discovered, they very quickly put him to death. His body was quartered and burnt. So died Ulrich Zwingli, as the inscription over the door of his house in Zurich says "for truth and for his faith." The defeat of Cappel was a terrible blow to Zurich and to Protestantism. It would have been its death-blow, but for the fact that Protestantism had become so great a movement that the death of no one man could check it. God fortunately raised up a man, in every way fitted to be Zwingli's successor, in Henry Bullinger, of whom we will speak later.

VII. *Zwingli's Character and Doctrines.*

So lived, so died the great founder of the Reformed Churches. He was of all the Reformers the most modern in his views, and as time rolls on, his life and character are being better understood. He was by no means faultless. He made mistakes,—many of them,—though some of them were mistakes due to his age. There were none of the Reformers who were faultless and who made no mistakes. However, in spite of them, and rising above them, Zwingli appears as a great character and a mighty force. He was one of the four great pillars of the Reformation: Luther, Melancthon and Calvin being the other three. His greatness was many-sided. He was great as a thinker,* as a theologian, as a poet, as a patriot, as a statesman, and as an orator,— and all these were consecrated in the highest way to the cause of the Reformation. His was a great missionary spirit and he did not rest until most of German Switzerland had become Protestant.

His doctrinal position may be now defined as a "liberal Calvinism."

1. He strongly held to the *supremacy of Scripture.*
2. He held to the doctrine of *election*, as did all the

* In nine years he published about eighty works.

Reformers, even Luther. They emphasized this doctrine, because in their reaction against the Catholic doctrine of justification by works, they held to justification by faith. And as man's works could not save, then God alone could save and he did it by electing them. But Zwingli was broad and liberal in his Calvinism. He held that all infants were saved, and also that there was a possibility of salvation for some of the heathen, as Socrates and Seneca; for his love for the classics had liberalized his theological views. In holding this, he gave the death-blow to the doctrine of baptismal regeneration. And while strict Calvinists hold that Christ died for the elect, Zwingli held that He died for all.

But he did not live long enough to fully co-ordinate these doctrines into a system, for he died in middle life. On the doctrine of justification by faith he agreed with Luther, but his emphasis was different. He emphasized the *cause* of justification, namely, the death of Christ, while Luther emphasized the *result*, namely, justification. He says in his Confession to Emperor Charles V, "For this is the one sole mediator between God and men, the God and man Christ Jesus." Luther's doctrine was based on Galatians, Zwingli's on Hebrews (7:28 and 10:10). This emphasis of Zwingli's on the "Ransom of Christ" led him to hold at first to the memorial view of the Lord's Supper, though toward the end of his life he inclined toward the higher Calvinistic view.

VIII. *The Life of Leo Juda.*

This sketch of the life of Zwingli would not be complete without referring to his helper at Zurich, Leo Juda. It was at the feet of Prof. Thomas Wyttenbach at Basle that Zwingli and Leo Juda, born in southwestern Germany, 1482, first met. With Zwingli he drank in the Evangelical teachings of Wyttenbach, and in his life he somewhat followed Zwingli, going first to Einsedeln and then to Zurich, as pastor of St. Peter's Church. In the second Zurich disputation in 1523, Juda appeared as Zwingli's helper and debated against the mass. He also aided Zwingli in his correspondence and his preaching, and, when Zwingli was away from Zurich, acted as the head of the church. He was a fine scholar, and greatly helped Zwingli in the publication of the first German Bible after the Reformation. This was published at Zurich in 1530, four years before Luther's translation appeared. In it, Zwingli and Juda utilized Luther's translation as far as he had gone, but added other translations of their own, as of the Prophets.

When the Protestants were defeated at Cappel in 1531, his life was in great danger, because of the reaction that took place at Zurich against the Protestants. As he stood next to Zwingli in the Church, he was held somewhat responsible for the defeat. A colonel came to town for the express purpose of killing him, and was only prevented by Juda's friends so crowding around the man that he could not do it. The danger was so great that Leo Juda did not dare go out of his house. One night some of the women came and begged him to leave the house disguised as a woman. But he refused, and, buckling on his armor, walked through the main street to the house of a friend where the Protestants protected him. He stayed there until the storm was over. He was called to be Zwingli's successor, but declined. When Bullinger was called to that position, Juda was ever his right-hand man.

His greatest work for the Zurich Church was his preparation of two catechisms, that the children might be instructed in the faith,—a larger catechism in 1534, and a shorter one in 1541. In the first of these the catechumen asks the question and the minister gives the answer. But this was reversed in all later Reformed catechisms. They were widely introduced into other cantons, and even into other lands, and other catechisms as Calvin's were based on them. He died June 19, 1542, greatly honored. Time fails to speak of Zwingli's other helpers at Zurich, as Myconius, the schoolmaster, Pellican, the professor of

Hebrew, and also Christopher Froschouer, who published Zwingli's works, and who published so many Bibles that he was a whole Bible Society in himself. His missionary work in the sale and spread of his Bibles was very remarkable. We must also not forget to call attention to Bibliander, the successor of Zwingli, and the learned professor of Hebrew at Zurich, who urged missions to the Mohammedans and Jews (1546 and 1553) in his works and who for a time wanted to go as a missionary to the Mohammedans.

IX. *The Name of Ecolampadius.*

John Ecolampadius (or Œcolampadius, as the Germans have it) has never received his due at the hands of church historians. Perhaps his great modesty had something to do with it; but he was as great as he was modest. His name was in the German "Hausschein," which he, after the custom of his time, latinized into Ecolampadius. The word means "the light of the house," and Ecolampadius was a great light in God's House. Though in his modesty he was often in his own eyes only a rush-light, yet he was a "burning and shining light," as was John the Baptist.

X. *His Birth and Conversion.*

He was born at Weinsberg in southern Germany in 1482. He studied theology at the Universities of Heidelberg and Tübingen. As priest he came to Basle in 1515 just as the great scholar and humanist, Erasmus arrived; and there he entered the select circle of the learned, led by Erasmus. He was so fine a scholar in Hebrew that Erasmus utilized him a great deal to help him. Indeed, Erasmus declared that he was the best Hebrew scholar of his day, next to Reuchlin. Erasmus, though he bitterly attacked the abuses of the Catholic church, yet never became a Protestant. He was too timid. But what Erasmus did not do, as we shall later see, Ecolampadius did,—he began the Reformation. The old proverb was that "Erasmus laid the egg of the Reformation, but Luther hatched it." As far as Basle was concerned, Ecolampadius, and not Luther hatched it. When he first arrived at Basle he was not yet a Reformer, though his great seriousness was fertile ground for it. In 1516 he returned to his home, but in 1518 he is again at Basle at the earnest request of Erasmus, so as to aid him in the publication of the second edition of the New Testament. Then for a short time he was pastor at Augsburg in Germany. When Luther's theses were scattered over Germany, he was greatly influenced by them. Then to the surprise of his friends, he suddenly entered the cloister near Augsburg in 1520. But he soon became disgusted with the life of the monks and left the cloister, saying, "I have put off the monk, and have found Christ." Where to go, he knew not. He was then called in 1522 as pastor at Ebernberg, by Count Francis of Sickingen, who inclined to the Reformation. But when that prince lost his principality, Ecolampadius had to leave.

XI. *The Beginnings of the Reformation at Basle.*

At the end of 1522 he is again at Basle, where he became vicar of St. Martin's Church. But now, instead of Erasmus having the greatest influence over him, it is Zwingli, whose reformatory movements at Zurich had by this time attracted attention. His learning soon led to his becoming a lecturer in the university, in which he began to reveal his Evangelical leanings. In 1525 he was advanced so as to be head-priest at St. Martin's Church at Basle, which gave him great influence and greater freedom to preach the Gospel. There came a reaction against Protestantism in 1525, so that even some of his friends urged him to leave. But he kept on quietly but firmly introducing the Reformation; and in November, 1525, he introduced the Protestant Lord's Supper in his own church.

XII. *The Conference at Baden.*

It was the disputation at Baden, May 2, 1526, that brought Ecolampadius' ability into prominence. To that disputation the Catholics had brought the most eloquent opponent of the Reformation, Eck. He claimed to have already crushed Martin Luther at the Leipsic Disputation, and he expected to crush Protestantism at this. The cause of Protestantism was in great peril unless some strong leader should arise. Zwingli was the one who could have led. But this Conference at Baden was intended to inveigle him there so that the Catholics might imprison, and perhaps kill him, and so the Zurich Council forbade his going. Fortunately for the Protestants, Ecolampadius was there and proved to be the man of the hour. He debated with Eck with great power, on the mass, on prayers to Mary and the saints, and on images. He produced a profound impression even on the Catholics. He matched Eck in argument so that some of Eck's friends declared that "Ecolampadius is not vanquished by argument, but by vociferations," and some of the Catholics declared: "If only this pale man were on our side." His host, who was a Catholic, declared that if he was a heretic, he was a very pious one, for he said that Ecolampadius was always engaged in study and in prayer.

XIII. *Progress of the Reformation at Basle.*

After the Conference at Baden, Ecolampadius went back to Basle to continue his work of reforming that city. He published a Protestant form of worship, and, unlike Zwingli at Zurich, introduced congregational singing. But the progress was slow, because the city council always tried to mediate between Catholics and Protestants. When a new bishop of Basle was elected in 1527 and entered the city in great pomp, Ecolampadius wrote to Zwingli "Our cause hangs on a thread." In 1528 he attended the Conference of Bern. The fact that the canton of Bern had decided to become Reformed greatly affected Basle, but still the city council tried to conciliate. However, certain events brought matters to a crisis. On Good Friday, 1528, some Protestant zealots, without the knowledge of Ecolampadius, went to his Church of St. Martin's, and took away all the images from the altar. On Easter Monday, they did the same in the Church of the Augustines. The city council put five of them in prison, but soon released them.

THE REFORMATION AT BASLE 33

The controversy, however, continued. The priests in the cathedral inveighed against the Reformers as heretics and knaves; and the Protestant pastors in the other churches preached against the superstitions in the cathedral. Burgomaster Meyer led the Reformed, Burgomaster Meltinger led the Catholics. On December 23, 1528, 300 of the citizens met in the Carpenter Guild Hall and drew up a petition to the council for Protestantism. As they took the petition to the council the Catholics met them, and, brandishing swords and lances, tried to bar their way. Nevertheless the Reformed carried it to the council. Meltinger refused to receive the petition, but Meyer received it and brought it before the council. Still the council failed to act. But then there came rumors throughout the city that Zurich and Bern were about to send help to the Reformed, and Austria, to the Catholics. The result was that both parties armed, and Christmas night was spent by both parties under arms. This strained condition continued until February 8, 1529. By that time it became evident that the Protestants were in control of the situation. Meltinger fled across the Rhine, as did the other Catholic members of the council. Then some of the Protestants in passing the cathedral pulled out an image, which broke into pieces as it fell on the pavement. They then pulled out others. "I am surprised," said Erasmus ironically, "that the saints perform no miracles to save themselves, for formerly they worked great prodigies for much smaller offenses." The Protestants continued this casting out of images in the other churches. On Ash Wednesday of that year, a number of images were burned, so that some wags said "The idols are really keeping their Ash Wednesday to-day." Then the city council gave orders that thereafter there should be no masses said in Basle, and that was the end of Catholicism there. Ecolampadius, who for years had been faithfully preaching the Gospel, was after this victory transferred to the cathedral and made head of the church. During all this time Zwingli, with true missionary zeal, encouraged

Ecolampadius by his correspondence and sympathy.

VIV. *Ecolampadius' Last Days.*

When the Marburg Conference met in 1529, he went there with Zwingli. Zwingli was, however, the leader of the Reformed in that Conference. When the catastrophe of the Swiss Reformation occurred in 1531 and Zwingli was killed on the battlefield of Cappel, Ecolampadius was greatly grieved and worried. The Church at Zurich called him to succeed Zwingli, but he declined. He soon after died, November 29, 1531, after a brief illness. As the pastors of the city gathered round his dying bed, he asked of one who came in "What is the news?" "Nothing," was the reply. "But I will tell you something new," was his answer. His friends waited in astonishment and Ecolampadius continued "In a short time I shall be with the Lord Jesus." He died with the words "Lord Jesus help me." Yes, "there was light at eventide" with him as his life went out. He had been "a burning and shining light" for the Reformation. Intellectually he stands in the front rank of the Reformers, and is the twin-Reformer of Zwingli, as Melancthon was of Luther. A man who could write a book which was so powerful as to make a scholar like Melancthon change his view about the Reformed in regard to doctrine of the Lord's Supper is not a tyro; yet that is what Ecolampadius did in his work entitled "The Dialogue." In learning he ranks with Zwingli, for he was one of the most learned in the Church Fathers.

XV. *Vadian and St. Gall.*

While Zwingli was busy at Zurich, the light of the Reformation spread to other cantons and cities. Just as the Alpine sun-rise, as seen from the Rigi mountain, so beautifully lights one snow-capped peak after another; so the cities of Switzerland were lit one after the other with the light of the new day of the Reformation. The first to accept it was St. Gall, 1527, followed by Bern, 1528, and Basle, 1529. The Reformer of St. Gall was Vadian; of Bern, Haller; and of Basle, Ecolampadius.

VADIAN'S EARLY LIFE

Vadian was the great *Layman* of the Swiss Reformation. The conversion of St. Gall to Protestantism was one of the most notable victories of the Reformation, for St. Gall and Einsedeln were the two great centres of Catholicism in German Switzerland. In the seventh century, Gallus, the British missionary who held a purer, simpler worship than the Romish, had founded a monastery at St. Gall. But by the sixteenth century this monastery had become full of Catholic superstitions. That this great abbey should become Protestant was one of the surprises of the Reformation. Nowhere in the Reformation were the lines more clearly drawn than at St. Gall between town and gown, that is, between the citizens of the town and the robed clergy of the abbey. And all this great victory was due to the ability and influence of this Reformer of St. Gall, Joachim Vadian, or Vadianus. Vadian's real name was Von Watt, but according to the custom of his age, he latinized his name into Vadianus. Like James Watt, who discovered steam, and by that discovery made this a new world; so Joachim Von Watt discovered Protestantism, and by it made St. Gall a new city.

XVI. *Vadian's Birth and Education.*

He was born at St. Gall, December 28, 1484, the same year as Zwingli. In 1502 he went to the university of Vienna, where he remained sixteen years, first as a student and then as professor. While at the university two things prepared him to be a Reformer. The first was his acceptance of humanism; the second was his meeting with Zwingli, who was his fellow-student there. As they were from the same district of Switzerland, they became very close friends. Vadian revealed great ability, taking two degrees at the university in four years. Later, in 1510, he began lecturing in the university with great acceptance. He also began writing poems and the Emperor of Germany was so pleased with them that, in 1514, he made Vadian Poet Laureate. Two years later, Vadian, though only 32 years of age, was elevated to be rector, or head of the university of Vienna. That a small Swiss city should produce the rector of a great university at such a youthful age made St. Gall very proud of him. And this helped him to gain so great an influence there, that he was later able to swing the city to Protestantism.

Vadian's natural love for the sciences led him to study medicine, and in 1517 he took the degree of doctor of medicine. In 1518 he left Vienna on account of the plague, expecting to return; but when he came home to St. Gall, the city honored him by appointing him city-physician, and in 1520 made him a member of the city council. The rest of his life was spent in his native city. And there was a providence in it; for God brought him home to begin the Reformation in his own city.

XVII. *Preparations for the Reformation.*

When he came back to St. Gall there was no sign of the Reformation. The city was closely controlled by the abbey and was full of papal superstitions. When Zwingli began his work at Zurich, St. Gall soon heard of it, and Vadian was the leader in the movement toward it. Thus he gathered together those who were inclined to be Evangelical and gave them lectures on the Acts of the Apostles. He aimed by this to show them what the early church was like. These lectures were never published, but are in the city library of St. Gall. He also tried to get Evangelical ministers and schoolmasters for his city. Zwingli with his missionary spirit encouraged Vadian and this Evangelical movement at St. Gall with all his power. In 1523 Vadian showed his sympathy for the Reformers by going to the second great disputation at Zurich, where he was made one of the presidents of the Conference.

But still St. Gall had not been shaken by the Reformation. How was it possible that a city, chained so close to Rome by the abbey, should become Reformed. The Protestant movement began in 1524. A young man who had been born in St. Gall, named John Kessler, had gone away to Basle to study for the priesthood. There he met Erasmus and became a humanist. And there he also heard Ecolampadius and became a Protestant. He came back to St. Gall, but as he had lost faith in the priesthood, he started as a saddler's apprentice. A number of men, inclined to the Evangelical doctrines, came to him and asked him, though only a layman, to give them expositions of the Bible. And soon hearers streamed to him from all parts of the town. The rulers of the abbey, alarmed, brought complaint against him to the Swiss Diet. (They played on his name, calling him "Kettlemender.") The Diet warned St. Gall that a layman had no right to preach. He was, therefore, called before the council of St. Gall, which ordered him to give up his Bible lectures. But lo, it did something better. It ordered three preaching services each week in the Churches. And though Kessler gave up his Bible lectures, they were continued by a converted monk of the abbey, named Schorant, and the attendance became so great that his followers asked that St. Mangen's Church should be opened to them. As the abbot had its doors locked, Schorant mounted the wall of the churchyard and preached to them. But it was still winter, and too cold for open-air services. So, finally, on Sunday, February 2, 1525, the city council opened the St. Lawrence Church, the leading church of the city, and there Kessler preached.

XVIII. *Introduction of the Reformation into St. Gall.*

In 1526 Vadian was made burgomaster of the city, and was re-elected to that office eight times, continuing in it until his death. On Easter, 1527, the first Protestant Lord's Supper was celebrated in the St. Lawrence Church. This signified that the city had become Reformed. At the beginning of 1528 Vadian attended the great Conference at Bern, and was one of its presidents. Soon after that, the Protestants carried the city council at St. Gall, and so gained entire control of the city. In 1528 St. Gall made a league with the Protestant cantons of Zurich and Bern, thus declaring her full allegiance to Protestantism. At this the abbot of the monastery became alarmed and fled from the city, and Zurich closed it as a Catholic institution. On March 2, 1529, Zili, a Protestant schoolmaster, held the first Protestant service in the abbey, at which 4,000 persons were present and Protestant services were held in the abbey for four years. Vadian was also busy doing missionary work for Protestantism in the neighboring canton of Appenzell, so that in 1530 a synod was organized at which Zwingli was present.

But the fateful year 1531 brought defeat to the Protestants, as Zwingli was killed at the Battle of Cappel. Vadian, when he heard of it, fell into a fever because of anxiety, saying, "Oh, poor congregation of St. Gall." And well he might be deeply anxious, for the act of Zurich in taking the abbey at St. Gall, and allowing Protestant services there, had greatly angered the Catholics. Vadian could now expect reprisals, and they came. The two abbeys of Einsedeln and St. Gall were given back to the Catholics, and have been in their hands ever since. The city of St. Gall was ordered to pay 1,000 florins for the injury done to the abbey, of which Zurich was to pay 400.

XIX. *Vadian's Later Years and Character.*

Thus peace came, but the friction between the Catholic abbey and the Protestant town continued. In 1531 the Catholics scattered pamphlets throughout the town against the Protestants. In reply the city council forbade the citizens to attend the services of the abbey. In 1542 Kessler, who had started the Reformation at St. Gall, was called back to St. Gall as pastor, and later, in 1571, he became the head minister or antistes of the Church. He died in 1578. Before he died Vadian had passed away, April 6, 1551.

Such was the man of whom Zwingli said: "I know no Swiss that equals him." Both Calvin and Beza recognized him as a man of real piety and equally real learning. He was a many-sided man. He was a professor and poet in his youth, and a physician in his later life. He also wrote history, but he excelled in geography. He was

VADIAN'S DEATH

one of the leading geographers of his time. But, greatest and best of all, he was an earnest Christian. He stands out as the great Layman of the Swiss Reformation. The other Reformers were ministers, or, if they were at first laymen, they became preachers. Not so Vadian; he was a Reformer and yet a layman. His prominence is shown by his appointment to be president at the religious Conferences at Zurich in 1523 and at Bern in 1528. And when the two great leaders of the Swiss Reformation, Zwingli and Ecolampadius, were cut off by death within about a month of each other, Vadian was then looked up to by the Protestants of Switzerland as their leader. In the negotiations after the sad defeat at Cappel in 1531, Vadian guided the Protestants.

The Reformed Church has always emphasized the work of laymen, and given them an equal seat with the ministers in the church courts. What great laymen the Reformed Church had in the Reformation, as Admiral Coligny in France, William of Orange in Holland, Elector Frederick III in Germany, and others. What kind of laymen and church members does the Reformed Church have now? Are they worthy of those who have gone before, or are they only "degenerate sons of noble sires?" What an inspiration a man like Vadian should be to our church members, so true, so pure and so active in God's cause.

QUESTIONS

How was Zwingli a missionary?
Describe the Conference at Baden.
Describe the Conference at Bern.
What did Zwingli send to the Emperor at Augsburg?
How was Zwingli active in politics and missionary work?
Describe the First Cappel War, and what did Zwingli write in connection with it?

What led to the Second Cappel War?
Describe the defeat at Cappel and Zwingli's death.
What was the effect of the defeat at Cappel?
Describe Zwingli's character and theology.
What was Leo Juda's early association with Zwingli?
How did Juda help Zwingli at Zurich?
Describe his later life.
Who was Ecolampadius, and what did his name mean?
Describe his birth and conversion.
What were his relations to Erasmus?
Describe his early ministry at Basle.
What part did he take in the Conference at Baden?
How did the Reformation ultimately triumph at Basle?
Describe his last years.
What was the significance of his character to us?
How did the Reformation spread through Switzerland?
Why was St. Gall so difficult to make Protestant?
Where was Vadian educated?
What led him to become a Reformer?
What did he do at first to introduce the Reformation?
Who was the young man who first began preaching in St. Gall, and what were its effects?
To what high position in the city was Vadian elected?
When was Protestantism officially introduced into St. Gall?
What Protestant service was held at the Abbey?
What results did the defeat of Cappel have on St. Gall?
What was Vadian's character?
What does his life teach us?

GENEVA
To the Left in the Distance is Mt. Blanc. The Cathedral is to be Seen to the Right

CHAPTER III

THE COMPLETION OF THE REFORMATION IN GERMAN SWITZERLAND BY HALLER AND BULLINGER AND ITS BEGINNING IN FRENCH SWITZERLAND BY FAREL

I. *Haller's Youth and Education.*

Berthold Haller, the Reformer of Bern, is an illustration of the way in which a man of ordinary ability can become great, because he remained steadfast in an hour of crisis. He was born in southern Germany in 1492. He went to school with Melancthon at Pforzheim, in Germany, where they became close friends. He was called to Bern in 1513 as an assistant in the school of his former teacher, Rubellus. By his industry and worth of character he made many friends. Gradually the way to enter the priesthood opened before him, for one of the guilds, the bakers, elected him as their chaplain; and in 1517 he became apostolic notary, also an ecclesiastical position. The movements towards Protestantism had their forerunner in the influence of Nicholas Manuel, one of the leaders of Bern, a poet, a painter, a warrior and a statesman. But more important for Haller was the coming to Bern of Thomas Wyttenbach, Zwingli's teacher, who in 1515 became priest in the cathedral at Bern. In the latter part of Wyttenbach's stay in Bern, Haller lived with him. It is easy to see what an influence for the Reformation Wyttenbach would have on him. Wyttenbach left Bern in 1520 to become a Reformer of his birthplace, Biel, a town west of Bern, though he later returned to Bern and died there.

II. *Beginning of the Reformation at Bern.*

In 1520 Haller was elected a canon at the cathedral.

His eloquent preaching gained him influence. His sermons revealed an Evangelical tendency. When he heard what Zwingli was doing at Zurich he greatly rejoiced. In 1521 he visited Zwingli at Zurich, and began a friendship which lasted until the latter's death. But his preaching aroused hatred, and the Catholics began to call him a heretic. He preferred peace, but circumstances forced him on. In February, 1522, two Fastnacht plays were given at Bern. These boldly revealed the great corruption of the Church and helped to hasten the Reformation. Haller began, like Zwingli, to preach on the Gospel of Matthew, verse by verse. In June, 1523, the city council ordered that only the Gospel should be preached, and by November 20 of that year the nuns left the convent. But in 1524 the priest Meier, who sympathized with him, was compelled to leave Bern. That left Haller the only Protestant among the priests. His position was made more difficult by the fact that on April 7, 1525, the council issued a new decree restoring the Catholic worship, though with a few changes. Haller was thus hindered and threatened on every side, yet he remained firm.

In 1526 Haller attended the Conference at Baden. He found everything arranged to prejudice the case against the Evangelicals. With Ecolampadius he took part in the debate, and attacked the doctrine of the mass as a sacrifice. He had not the learning of Ecolampadius, but he made an able defense from Scripture. When he returned to Bern he found himself in a dilemma. The little council had ordered him, under pain of dismissal, to again perform the mass (which he had not done for half a year), because this had been decreed by the Conference at Baden. The matter was carried up to the great council. Here there was a stormy session, so that the rumor went abroad that they had come to blows. Haller begged them to be at peace, and said he would rather leave the city than cause such strife. But he was vindicated by being reappointed preacher at the cathedral.

THE BERN CONFERENCE 43

And now at last the Evangelical reform began really to grow in Bern. Haller's preaching produced a profound impression. The plague came in 1526 and solemnized the people, and that helped the Protestant cause. His labors became so great that he begged for an assistant, and finally gained one in Francis Kolb. So there were now two Evangelical preachers in the city of Bern. In 1527 the Reformed party gained the control of the great council, and it ordered that the Word of God should be preached. Still there was a conflict about the mass, as some congregations still observed it. Then came the controversy about the marriage of priests and about monasteries. Haller wrote to Zwingli at that critical time for advice. Zwingli warned him not to go too fast in setting aside the mass, until the hearts of the people revealed a great desire for the Lord's Supper. So it was finally decided that there should be a religious disputation at Bern, January 6, 1528, to settle these questions.

III. *The Conference at Bern.*

This Conference was attended by a large number of foreign delegates, who came from the other cantons and even from southern Germany. More than 100 delegates left Zurich for Bern, guarded by 300 armed men. All the leaders of the Reformed were there; Bucer and Capito came from Strassburg, Zwingli from Zurich, and Ecolampadius from Basle. They came with the great missionary impulse to convert the large canton of Bern to Protestantism. In the discussion of the theses at the Conference, either Haller or Kolb always began the debate on each thesis, but, as we have before said, the commanding character at the Conference was Zwingli.

An interesting incident is told concerning Zwingli at this Conference. On Sunday, January 19, Zwingli went up into the pulpit and preached on the articles in the Apostles' Creed on Christ's ascension, session, and second coming. "These three articles," says Zwingli, "contradict the mass." While he was thus preaching against the mass, a priest attempted to celebrate mass at one of the side altars. But as he listened to Zwingli, he stopped in astonishment at Zwingli's words. And suddenly, in the presence of the whole congregation, he tore off his priest's robes, and, throwing them on the altar, he exclaimed: "Unless the mass rests on a more solid foundation, I can celebrate it no longer."

This dramatic conversion of this priest produced a most profound impression on the council and the city, and undoubtedly helped the Reformed to gain the victory at the Conference. The result of this Conference was that the great council, on January 27, 1528, ordered that in the city all masses should be stopped and all images cast out. On February 7, 1528, it ordered the same for the whole canton. Haller also received assistant ministers, who were Evangelical, to help him. In April, 1528, the Protestant Lord's Supper was first celebrated, and thus the great canton of Bern became Reformed. But the influence of this Conference not only wheeled the large canton of Bern into the Protestant column, but opened the way for the introduction of the Protestant Gospel into the cantons of French Switzerland, as we shall see when we take up Farel's life. We shall then see how Bern constantly worked to introduce and protect Protestantism in French Switzerland. Haller continued preaching the Gospel faithfully until his end came on the 25th of February, 1536. He had been a faithful witness for his Master, often standing alone for the Gospel amid much opposition and danger.

IV. *Henry Bullinger—His Birth and Education.*

Henry Bullinger belongs to the second generation of the Reformers. Those we have already described belonged to the first generation. Bullinger came in to complete in Zurich what Zwingli had begun. He was born July 18, 1504, at the little town of Bremgarten, west of Zurich. His life was evidently preserved for great purposes, for several times he was saved from death in his boyhood days.

At the age of twelve he went abroad to study. We have already spoken of humanism as one of the preparatory movements to the Reformation. We must here note another, the schools of the Brethren of the Common Life. The Brethren of the Common Life was an Order in the Catholic Church founded before the Reformation by spiritually-minded men, who longed for better things than they found in the Catholic Church of their day. They founded schools to prepare priests and monks for a higher, better ministry. The most famous of this Order was Thomas A'Kempis, whose "Imitation of Christ" reveals the deep piety of the man, though tinctured with monasticism. To one of the schools of the Brethren of the Common Life at Emmerich, in Holland, Bullinger went. There he received an excellent education. Like Luther, he sang in the streets and at the doors of private houses so as to gain money for his education.

After remaining there three years he went, in 1519, to the university of Cologne. This university was intensely Catholic, and bitterly opposed Protestantism, and yet in 1520 Luther's works were scattered abroad in Cologne, although the university declared them heretical. Bullinger felt the influence of this upheaval that was taking place around him, and with greater earnestness than ever he studied the early Fathers of the Church. He noted the difference between them and the Catholic doctrines of his time. Then he secretly read Luther's works, especially his "Babylonish Captivity." It seemed to him that Luther came nearer to the early Church Fathers than the Catholics of his day, especially because the Fathers founded themselves on the Bible rather than on the Church. So he secured a New Testament and read it. The result of it was that he gave up the previous plan of his life, which had been to join one of the strictest Orders of the monks, the Carthusians. In fact, he found that the whole Romish system was becoming distasteful to him. Then Melancthon's "Commonplaces," a work on theology, fell into his hands. This so impressed him that, in 1521 and 1522, he became a great student of the Bible, reading it day and night. Thus he gradually passed out of the Catholic Church. In 1522 he returned home to Switzerland.

V. *His Call to Zurich.*

But what should be do? His education had been for the monkhood, but now he must do something else. So he went to teaching, and in 1523 was rector of the cloister school at Cappel, and later, in 1528, became pastor at Cappel. In 1529 he became pastor at Bremgarten, where he was born. But in 1531, when Zurich was defeated at Cappel, he was compelled by the Catholic army to flee from Bremgarten, and found refuge in Zurich. He found everything there in confusion. The Catholic party was trying to manoeuvre things so as to bring Zurich back to Catholicism. The Protestants had no leader, for the reaction against Zwingli had compelled Leo Juda to hide himself. Things looked dark for the Protestants. While Zurich was waiting for the answer of Ecolampadius to become the head minister, Bullinger was invited to preach in the cathedral. He preached with such power that many thought him Zwingli risen from the dead. His youth made him unmindful of his danger. A contemporary said: "Only young Bullinger thunders." He was the kind of man that Zurich was looking for as antistes, or head minister; and when Ecolampadius declined that position, Bullinger was elected, though only 27 years of age. He proved to be the man of the hour. It was a great honor, but also a great responsibility for so young a man to be called to so prominent a place.

VI. *His Activity as Antistes.*

Fortunately he was a man of great courage, common sense, prudence and eloquence, so that he splendidly filled Zwingli's place. By his wisdom he destroyed the hopes of the Catholics for a reaction at Zurich, and by his firmness he rallied the Reformed. He soon became known all over Europe as the worthy successor of Zwingli. He was a man of great kindness of heart, and when the family of Zwingli was left in poverty by Zwingli's sudden death, he took them under his roof and raised the children as his own. He was also accustomed to take promising young men into his family in order to study for the ministry, and an interesting romance grew out of it. One of these young men was Rudolph Gualther, who fell in love with Zwingli's daughter, Regula, and later married her. Later Gualther became the successor of Zwingli and Bullinger as the antistes of the Church at Zurich. Bullinger proved himself a very wise administrator of the Church. He was also an eloquent preacher and a faithful pastor. He exerted a great influence on the city government, as he had the courage of his convictions. He was very watchful against the Catholics, preventing them from doing any work in Zurich that would undermine the Protestants.

VII. *The Tigurine Confession.*

He was also influential outside of Zurich. The Protestant cantons looked on him as their mediator. He was especially successful in welding the Reformed of French, or southern Switzerland, with those of German, or northern Switzerland. This was done in 1549, when Calvin and Bullinger drew up a creed called the Tigurine Confession,* in which they agreed on the doctrine of the Lord's Supper. In doing so Bullinger accepted Zwingli's later view, that there was a *spiritual* presence of Christ in the Lord's Supper. This view is familiarly called the Calvinistic, and holds that the Lord's Supper has not merely a *past* reference as in the memorial view, but brings a *present* spiritual blessing to those who have faith. Bullinger also drew up the Second Helvetic Confession, the most widely adopted of the Reformed confessions. He at first drew it up as his own personal creed, but when it was published it was adopted by all the Protestant cantons of Switzerland as their creed, and was afterward adopted by other Reformed churches, as Hungary, Bohemia, etc.

* Tigurine is derived from the word Zurich.

VIII. *His Missionary Spirit.*

He felt a deep interest in the spread of the Gospel everywhere. Thus he was deeply interested in the conversion of Italy. The Reformation had gained adherents in northern Italy, at Locarno, and he had aided them with his counsel and influence. A congregation of two hundred was organized by Beccaria. But Beccaria was driven away, and then the Protestants, in 1555, were summoned before the city council and ordered to become Catholics or leave the town in midwinter. They refused to recant, and were driven out at a season when all access to the Protestants on the northern side of the Alps was impossible. They fled to a neighboring valley belonging to the Swiss canton of the Grisons. But, as they were unsafe there, they, in the spring, before the Swiss passes were open, fled, men, women and children, over the snows of the St. Bernardino pass. They came to Coire, and then to Zurich, where Bullinger and the citizens, who had before fostered them, gave them a cordial welcome, and many of them settled there. Some of the most prominent families of Zurich to-day are descended from them. The fact is that the present prominence of Zurich as the largest of the Swiss cities is due to the silk industry which these Italian refugees brought with them there.

Bullinger was also deeply interested in the conversion of England to Protestantism. Many were his letters to the Evangelicals there, giving them encouragement and guidance. He watched every move there with the deepest solicitude. When the Protestants were driven out, he welcomed them to Zurich. One of the first to come was Hooper, later a bishop of the Anglican Church and founder of the low-church party in that Church. When Queen Mary came to the throne of England, and Hooper was imprisoned and put to death, Bullinger's letters to him in prison greatly strengthened him. Hooper, in dying, gave his glove to Bullinger, as a token of affection, and it was long preserved in the Bullinger family as a sacred relic. Many of the British ministers who fled from the Marian persecution came to Zurich. Bullinger gladly received them, and even opened a theological school for their young students. In 1558, after Queen Mary's death, they went back to England to re-found the Anglican Church, in which five of them became bishops. All this gave Bullinger great influence in that Church. Thus in many parishes the clergy were required to read his sermons, and his work, "The Ten Decades," was used in Oxford university as the guide in theology. As a sign of their gratefulness for his kindness, three of these bishops each presented silver cups to the Church of Zurich, and a finely embellished cup was sent by Queen Elizabeth in 1560 to Bullinger.* Bullinger also had an interesting correspondence with Lady Jane Grey, whose three Latin letters to him are among the gems in the Zwingli Museum at Zurich.

Bullinger reveals his missionary zeal in his correspondence. It, like that of Calvin's, became very great. Many, for instance, were the letters he wrote to the canton of the Grisons so as to make it Protestant. He was also deeply interested in the evangelization of Poland, and wrote many letters there. He thus exerted a wide influence all over Europe. His work was so large that finally, in 1575, his health gave way. On August 26 he bade good-bye to the ministers of Zurich, and on Saturday evening, September 17, 1575, he passed to his reward, after almost a half century of leadership in the Zurich Church and indeed of all the Reformed Churches. His death was greatly mourned all over Europe.

IX. *William Farel.*

William Farel was the picturesque character among the Reformers, for he was the great evangelist of the Reformation—the Elijah of the Alps—the John the Baptist, preparing the way of Jesus in many hearts. He was a mighty preacher with a tremendous voice—the Whitefield

* These are in the National Museum in Zurich.

of the Reformation. He excelled all the Reformers in daring courage, for it is said "he feared no man, only God." And he might also be called the great foreign missionary of the Reformation, because he went into territory that had never heard the Evangelical Gospel and evangelized it. The other Reformers were most of them mainly home missionaries, building up the church in their own cities or districts, as Zwingli in Zurich and Bucer in Strassburg. Calvin, too, was rather a home missionary, for he aimed to build up the church in Geneva. But Farel was a foreign missionary. To-day we call those whom we send to Catholic lands, as Latin America, foreign missionaries. If they are foreign missionaries, so was Farel, who, like them, evangelized in Catholic lands that knew not the Gospel. Everywhere that Farel went he preached and talked Christ to the people with true missionary zeal.

X. *Farel's Youth and Conversion.*

Farel was a Frenchman by birth, having been born (1489) at Gap, in the French Alps. As a boy he was fond of adventure. Into whatever he went, he went with his whole heart. So in his youth he was an intensely bigoted and superstitious papist; and when he later became a Protestant he put the same whole-heartedness into his work. As a youth he wanted to study, and so went to Paris. Fortunately for him, there was in the university at that time a professor who was to him what Wyttenbach had been to Zwingli,—Prof. James Lefevre, who, as we have seen, before either Luther or Zwingli, taught the doctrine of justification by faith, in his lectures. Under his teachings the eyes of this "rigid papist," Farel, were opened to the truth. There were at that time in Paris and the neighborhood a circle of pious spirits who were drawn together by their Evangelical views. They were protected by Margaret, the king's sister, who belonged to them. Farel joined himself to them, but he was too outspoken for them. They, though Evangelical, wanted to remain in the Catholic Church. But

Farel never stopped half-way in anything. The result was that he was compelled to leave France.

XI. *Farel in Exile.*

He fled to Basle; but what could he do there? He was bursting to tell the Gospel, but could not, as they spoke German and he spoke French. Finally God found a place for him in the District of Montbeliard, west of Basle. This was then under the control of the Duke of Wurtemberg of Germany, and was then opening to the Gospel. Ecolampadius ordained him at Basle in July, 1524, and sent him to Montbeliard to labor. His preaching soon caused a sensation, for there was always a sensation when Farel was about. Many heard and believed. As he was walking on the banks of the little river that flows through the town of Montbeliard on a Catholic festival day, he met a Catholic procession crossing the bridge over the river. They were reciting prayers, and were led by two priests bearing the image of the saint. His blood boiled at the sight of such idolatry. Unable to restrain himself, he boldly advanced, and, grasping the image from the hands of the priests, he threw it over the bridge into the river. Then he turned to the surprised crowd and said, "Poor idolaters, will you never cease from your idolatries?" It would have gone hard with Farel, for he would have been mobbed by the procession, had not an incident saved him. The priests, surprised and horror-stricken, for the moment lost their presence of mind. Then some one cried out, "The image is drowning," as if an image of wood could sink and be drowned. This diverted the attention of the crowd from Farel to the image. They rushed to save the saint in the water, and in the excitement Farel escaped. But he had done a most daring thing; and yet we will find that he was constantly doing such things. The duke, however, was compelled to leave Montbeliard, and so Farel had to leave. He went back to Basle, then to Strassburg, where for fifteen months he preached to French exiles. He was waiting for an opportunity to preach the Gospel to Frenchmen, and finally the opportunity came.

XII. *Farel at Aigle.*

His field was to be French Switzerland, and there, in his own French language, he could preach his Gospel. Bern had been capturing the French districts north of Lake Geneva. At the southeastern end of this district, in the valley of the Rhone, was the town of Aigle. At the suggestion of Haller, the Reformer at Bern, Farel went there in December, 1526, but disguised as a schoolmaster, under the name of Ursinus. He gathered the children and taught them, and he also taught them the Bible and Christ. Then he went further and began teaching the parents against Romish errors, as purgatory and intercession of the saints. When he had gained their respect, he announced himself as William Farel, and showed his appointment by the government of Bern to be their preacher. It happened there was a priest there who was afraid to attack Farel because of his great eloquence. So he went to a neighboring village, and from the pulpit denounced Farel, declaring that the devil preached through Farel. He then went back to Aigle, and on his way met Farel, who had heard what the priest had said. "Did you preach against me?" asked Farel, "and say that the devil spoke through me?" You must make good your statement, for I am ready to stake my life in defense of my doctrines." The monk began to bluster and denounce Farel, and a crowd began to gather. Farel still demanded proof from him, and took advantage of the crowd to give them some of the Gospel. The friar, pale and flushed by turns, took off his cap and, tramping it under foot, said: "I wonder the earth does not open and swallow you up." One of the bystanders took the monk by the sleeve and said: "Listen to him as he has listened to you." The monk, half-dead with fright, said to the man who held his sleeve: "Thou art excommunicated." At this the town was in an uproar. The result was that Farel, being backed by the government at Bern, compelled the monk to publicly apologize. For the Bern authorities always tried to spread Protestantism.

XIII. *Farel in Neuchatel.*

Farel now turned to a larger field than Aigle. Protected by Bern, he went to evangelize in the large district of Vaud, south of Bern. He preached at Morat, and gained some disciples, and at Lausanne, but was driven out. On a December day, 1529, a frail boat was seen to cross the lake of Neuchatel to its western coast. In it was Farel, who wanted to preach the Gospel in this entirely Romish district of Neuchatel. Not Caesar when he crossed the Rubicon, with the empire of Rome on his shoulders, carried a greater responsibility than did Farel; for the salvation of the whole of French Switzerland was resting upon him. No foreign missionary now traveling on a steamer over the ocean was more really a missionary than he in this boat.

He landed at the village of Serrieres, about three miles south of the town of Neuchatel. He knew that the priest there was favorable to the Gospel, and he asked if he could preach in his church. The priest replied that the bishop had forbidden Farel's preaching in any of the churches. But he added that "the bishop had laid no injunction against preaching on the rocks and in the open air." So Farel, taking the hint, mounted a gravestone beside the door of the church and preached the first Protestant sermon in that district. That stone became the cornerstone of the Reformed Church of the canton of Neuchatel, all of whose inhabitants are now Protestants.

But the people in the town of Neuchatel, having heard that Farel was near, sent for him to come to their city. So at a fountain at the foot of the citadel hill he preached his first sermon. At first there was some disorder. "Throw him into the fountain," "Beat out his brains," were cries that were heard. But Farel was a preacher who feared neither drowning nor beating. So he continued preaching to ever-increasing audiences. Then he went back across the lake to the eastern shore to fill the whole district with his doctrines. The priests there became so alarmed at his presence that a humorous scene took place. In one of the towns, while the priest was at the high altar of the church saying mass, Farel entered unobserved. He went up into the pulpit and began to preach. The priest, when he heard Farel's voice and recognized him, was so frightened that he did not finish chanting the mass, but ran out of the church. Then Farel preached to the congregation, and they tore out the images and the altars, and made the church Protestant. By the middle of the year 1530 Farel returned to the town of Neuchatel, and the number of Protestants greatly increased. Matters came to a climax on Sunday, October 23. As Farel was preaching in one of the down-town churches, his congregation took him and climbed the steep street up the hill to the castle and to the cathedral. The canons and priests tried to stop them, but in vain. They forced their way through the crowd and entered the cathedral. They placed Farel in the pulpit, and he preached one of his most effective sermons. When he was through, they knocked down the images, crucifixes and altars; and the traveler who visits Neuchatel to-day will see in the cathedral an inscription, in large letters: "On October 23, 1530, idolatry was overthrown in this church by the citizens."

XIV. *Farel at Vallengin.*

Just before the last event, Farel went, in company with a young Protestant named Anthony Boyve, to the town of Vallengin, a few miles west of Neuchatel. The priest was about to chant the mass, when Farel entered the pulpit and began preaching. While he was preaching, the priest and his choir were chanting the mass. Suddenly Boyve, seeing that the mass was beginning to be preferred to the sermon, rushed up to the priest, and, snatching the host from his hands, cried out, "This is not the God you should worship.

He is above, in heaven." The audience was awed by this, and Farel took advantage of the silence to preach. But the priests and their party rushed to the tower and rang the alarm bell. This caused the whole town to gather. Farel and Boyve would have been killed had they not retired. And as they were trying to go back to Neuchatel they were attacked with stones and clubs, and dragged, half dead, to the castle at Vallengin. "Drown them," said its owner, the countess; "throw them into the river, these Lutheran dogs, who have despised the host." Never was Farel nearer to death. But just then several persons arrived from Neuchatel and suggested caution, and so they were thrown into prison. But they so beat Farel that the bloodstains were on the walls there for six years. However, the Bernese had him freed, though he had to rest for a month to recover from his injuries.

XV. *Farel at Geneva.*

But Farel had his eyes on a greater conquest than Neuchatel. He wanted the city of Geneva, the largest in French Switzerland, to be won for Christ. He had been down (1532) to Italy to win the Waldenses to the Reformed. On his return he stopped at Geneva. Here he preached in his hotel, and it created a great sensation. He and his companion, Saunier, were brought before the city council, but when they found that Farel was protected by Bern, they ordered him out of town. Before he left, however, the Catholics proposed that a disputation should be held. They thus hoped to get Farel in their power and kill him. Farel, at this disputation, attempted to defend the Gospel, but he was spit upon and beaten. A gun was leveled at him and the priming flashed, but the gun did not go off. Farel turned and said, "Your toy does not alarm me. I am not to be shaken by a popgun." Farel then got away from the priests and managed to get out of town, by the aid of some friends who rescued him from the mob. But, although he left the city, a little band of believers remained, and one morning, just before sunrise, they met in a garden outside of one of the city gates, to celebrate the first Protestant Lord's Supper. They were in great danger, for if the priests had found out what they were doing, they would have been killed. But as the ceremony was taking place, the sun rose over Mount Blanc, and they took it as the sign from God of His blessing.

As it was too dangerous for Farel to go back to Geneva, he sent there a school teacher named Froment, to begin by teaching the Gospel as he had previously done at Aigle. Froment soon gathered a school and taught Protestantism. Finally his adherents led him to the Molard Square, where he held the first public Protestant service, preaching from a market stall. But an armed band of Catholics forced their way to Froment and took him away, so that it was with the greatest difficulty that he was saved. He, however, had to leave Geneva, and his school was broken up.

All now seemed lost in Geneva. But about Christmas, 1533, there came to Geneva a deputation from Bern that brought three preachers with it, Farel, Viret and Froment, and insisted that they be heard. When Lent came, 1534, the Bernese demanded that their preachers be heard publicly, as there were rumors abroad that the Protestant preachers kept in dark corners and dared not appear in the Churches. So Farel was placed in the Franciscan pulpit, and preached the first Protestant sermon preached in a Church there. When Whitsunday came, a Protestant communion was held, Farel administering it. As it was being held, it appeared for a moment as if there would be a disturbance, for a priest in full clerical dress walked in as if he would break up the service. While all held their breath, he walked up to the communion table, threw off his robes, and asked to be received as a Protestant. After this, gradually one church after another was opened to the Protestants.

On August 8, 1535, as Farel was on his way to preach in the Franciscan church, he was met by a strong body of men, who took him to the main church, the cathedral of

St. Peter, and from its pulpit he preached the old Protestant Gospel. Then they threw the images out of all the churches. Finally, on May 21, 1536, the citizens took the oath to support the Reformation.

XVI. *Farel and Calvin.*

Farel prayed to God to send him a helper, for the work had grown too large for him. God always hears such prayers. Two months after the Genevese had accepted Protestantism, in July, 1536, a young man came to Geneva, named John Calvin, already famous because he had written the best book on theology in the Reformation. Such a man Farel had been praying for. And when he heard that Calvin was in Geneva, he called at his hotel and urged him to stay. The wonderful story of Farel's call to Calvin will be given in the next chapter. The result of this conference was that Calvin decided to remain, and he became Farel's co-laborer. Gradually the younger became more famous than the older, because he was a man of superlative ability. Farel, however, was never jealous, but cordially worked with him. In this he sets a good example to many Christian workers to-day. Hand in hand these two Reformers labored to make Geneva a model city. They succeeded in getting very strict laws passed against gambling, swearing, dancing, etc. But the laws proved to be too severe, for there came a reaction against them. Finally a breach occurred. Calvin and Farel refused to administer the Lord's Supper by the use of unleavened bread and without proper church discipline. The result was that they were both ordered to leave the city within three days. They departed and went to Basle, where they separated in their life-work. Calvin went to Strassburg, and afterwards returned to Geneva. Farel went to Neuchatel, whose church was still greatly attached to him.

XVII. *Farel's Last Years at Neuchatel.*

Farel's life, after he became pastor at Neuchatel, was comparatively tame, compared with his earlier life. He was getting older, though he still had the same courage. Protestantism was also becoming better established, so that the scenes through which he had once gone did not need to be so often repeated. Yet the old missionary fire was in him. Thus in 1542 he went to Metz, and was urged to preach on the next Sabbath. A pulpit had been erected in the churchyard of the Dominicans, and from it he preached to a large audience. While he was preaching, two of the monks came and ordered him to be silent. As he paid no attention to them, they had the church bells rung. But Farel's wonderful voice rose above the din. The next day he preached to 3,000 hearers. The town council, however, became alarmed and stopped his services. Then he retired to the neighboring town of Gorze. When a monk was preaching on salvation through Mary, Farel arose in the audience and questioned his statements. But the women in the church handled him so severely that he nearly lost his life. On Easter many came there from Metz, and he celebrated the Lord's Supper with them. This greatly enraged the Catholics at Metz, and as Farel was celebrating the Lord's Supper, suddenly armed troops fell on them. Some were killed. Farel was wounded, but escaped. After a year's absence, he returned to Neuchatel. When he heard that Calvin was sick and would probably die, he went to Geneva with the thought, "Oh, that I might die with him." With tears and prayers, he bade Calvin a last farewell. But his restless spirit would not down. Just before his death he went to Metz to strengthen the Church. He preached with great power, but the effort was too much for him. He sank on his couch after the sermon, and was with great difficulty taken back to Neuchatel. There he died a few weeks later, September 13, 1565.

Thus died the great missionary of the Reformation. In season and out of season he was laboring for souls. His life should be an inspiration for missionary work. The secret of his success was that he was a mighty man of prayer. Often he would carry away his hearers in his prayers. When his enemies came to attack him, he sometimes prayed them into silence. Placed on his coat of arms was the motto, "What would I but that it were kindled." He, under God's Spirit, kindled a fire that has never been put out. O, that God would kindle by His Spirit such workers in the Church as Farel!

QUESTIONS

When did Haller first come to Bern and what position did he have?
Who there early influenced him toward Protestantism?
What did he do at the Conference at Baden?
What difficulties had he to overcome at Bern?
What was the effect of the Bern Conference?
What does Haller's life teach us?
Describe Bullinger's birth and boyhood.
Who were the "Brethren of the Common Life"?
How was he converted to Protestantism?
When he returned to Switzerland what did he do?
How did he come to be called as Zwingli's successor at Zurich?
What were his various activities in the Church?
What was his kindness to Zwingli's family?
What was the Tigurine Confession?
What was his missionary interest in the Italian Reformation?
What was his missionary interest in the English Reformation?
Describe his death.
What was Farel's significance among the Reformers?
Where was he born?
How was he converted to Protestantism?
When exiled, where did he go?
Why was he unable at first to preach?

What controversy had he with the Catholics at Montbeliard?
What controversy had he with the Catholics at Aigle?
Where did he preach at Serrieres?
How did he preach at Neuchatel, and what were its results?
How did he preach at Vallengin, and what were its results?
What was his first effort at Geneva?
What did Froment do in Molard Square?
What was his second effort at Geneva?
Who providentially came to Geneva to help him?
Why were Farel and Calvin compelled to leave Geneva?
Where did each go to?
Describe his preaching at Metz and vicinity.
Describe his last days.
What lesson does he teach us for missionary work?

FAREL'S CALL TO CALVIN
Calvin is to the Left, Farel to the Right. Out the Window is the Cathedral in which they Preached

CHAPTER IV

THE LIFE AND WORK OF JOHN CALVIN

I. *Introduction.*

John Calvin was the greatest genius of the Reformation. The only ones to dispute this place with him are Luther and Zwingli. Luther is the popular hero of the Reformation, especially among the Germans, and Luther's greatness cannot be disputed. But it was mainly the greatness of inspiration—that is, he was able to inspire others. He was also a genius in Bible translation. Zwingli, too, was a scholar, but he died too early to produce his best, that is, produce things in which to scholarship is added the matured ripeness of later life. Melancthon, too, was a great scholar, but his vacillations and his tendency to mediate detracted from his greatness. But Calvin was the genius because:

1. He was the great *theologian* of the Reformation. He sprang into fame at the early age of twenty-six, when he published his "Institutes of Theology," which was the greatest dogmatic work of the Reformation.

2. He was also the greatest *exegete* of the Reformation,—"the prince of commentators," as Spurgeon calls him. His careful, ripe judgment, his spiritual insight, his acute perception and his practical tact make his commentaries valuable even to-day.

3. He was the greatest teacher of *ethics* (or morality) in the Reformation. None of the early Lutherans compared with him in this subject, and Calvin was here the greatest among the Reformed.

4. And, finally, Calvin was the *great Church organizer* of the Reformation. Compared with him, Luther did little

to organize the Church; he left the princes do that. As a result of this carelessness about organization, the Lutheran Church in this country has virtually had to reorganize itself. Not so Calvin. He carefully laid the foundations of the Presbyterian Church government of the Reformed. It is strange that Calvin, who was so theoretic and logical, should also excel in such practical matters as Church organization. It reveals the universal character of his mind, which is one of the characteristics of genius. The great fault that has been found with Calvin has been his lack of heart, his intellectuality. He has been charged with being cold as an icicle. But that judgment is now being revised. Since his letters have been published, they reveal that, while Calvin was a man of very large head, he also had a very large heart; and Calvin is growing in the estimation of the world, as was shown in the recent 400th anniversary of his birth in 1909. Calvin would seem to be more of a builder-up of Churches already founded than a missionary, yet he had a true missionary spirit.

II. *His Birth and Youth.*

Calvin, it is to be remembered, belongs to the second generation of the great Reformers. The first generation was composed of Luther and Melancthon, Zwingli and Ecolampadius; but the last two were dead before Calvin began his work. He came to complete what they had begun. He was a Frenchman by birth, having been born at Noyon, in northern France, July 10, 1509. He was educated in the school of his birthplace. His association there with the noble family of Hangest, whose son Claude was his school-companion, gave to Calvin an acquaintance with the manners of polite society, which later distinguished him. In order to gain help to educate his son, Calvin's father secured for him a position in the Church. In those days the Catholic Church some times gave high positions even to boys. So John Calvin was appointed chaplain in the cathedral of Noyon at the age of twelve. Of course, he was not expected to preach. Some one else was found to perform his service at the altar. But he drew the salary. Six years later he added to this position the curacy of Pont-l-Eveque, the ancestral home of the Calvins. We see in all this how venial the Catholic Church had become; surely a reformation of the Church was needed. But this fact in Calvin's life reveals that he received the tonsure at the age of twelve, for otherwise he could not have held this office. And that was the only ordination, it seems absolutely certain, that Calvin ever had.

At the age of fourteen he was sent to Paris to study for the priesthood. He entered the College de la Marche, and there studied Latin under Cordier, from whom he gained his fine Latin style. Then he entered the College de Montaigu. He was an apt student and very religious, so much so that he was a censor of vices among his schoolmates. The Reformers as yet had no influence on him, for his teacher at this college was the great opponent of Lefevre and his Evangelical views. Calvin was still a stiff papist, especially as he had the priesthood in view.

But when he graduated, there came a change. His father insisted that he should study law instead of theology. So he was sent to the university of Orleans to study under the leading lawyer of France, Prof. de l' Estoile. Here he studied with great diligence. The burning of the midnight oil was his habit. By it he greatly enlarged his learning, but also laid the foundations of the ill-health with which he was later afflicted. While studying law he also emphasized the classics, and in studying them he came into contact with a Protestant professor, Melchior Wolmar, a German, who taught him Greek.

III. *Calvin Becomes a Protestant.*

Biographies of Calvin have heretofore held that Wolmar was the one who led him to become a Protestant. But later biographers tend to place his conversion later. The whole subject of Calvin's conversion is somewhat obscure. However, he always looked back with very grateful recollections to Wolmar. Wolmar removed from Orleans to Bourges, where Calvin also went to sit at the feet of a famous lecturer on law named Alciati. Alciati so lectured on law that it was not a mere matter of arbitrary detail, but he made it concrete instead of abstract, by illustrating it from history and literature. In the spring of 1531 occurred an event that changed all of Calvin's plans,—the death of his father. His father's death removed from him the pressure to study law. He, however, completed the law course and received his degree. And, though he no longer followed the law, there is no doubt that his legal studies greatly aided him afterward in his professorship and in the preparation of his work on theology. Calvin is always a logician, and he reveals his judicial balance of judgment in his excellent interpretations of the Bible in his Commentaries.

As soon as he had graduated from Bourges, he went to Paris to study the classics. He there became enamored with the new humanistic studies, and studied Greek and Hebrew. He also published (1532) his first book, a commentary on Seneca's "Treatise on Clemency," in which he reveals his remarkable ability and precocity. Written in Latin, its style has a peculiar clearness and brilliancy, and reveals the lawyer's grasp in its lucid presentation of the cogent argument. In it he shows remarkable familiarity with classic writings. It looked as if a new great leader of humanism had arisen to become the successor of Erasmus and Reuchlin, who had been its leaders. But in the book there are, as yet, no signs of Protestantism.

For providence had marked out for him a different career, namely, that of a Reformer. The study of the conversion of a great man is a very interesting one. We have watched Luther's and Zwingli's conversions. What was Calvin's? Was it of the heart or of the head? Here we come upon a very difficult subject,—one that has caused much discussion. One would expect that so intellectual a genius would have an intellectual conversion, and doubtless such it was; and yet, according to his statement, it was a sudden one. The old view was that Wolmer led to his conversion. It has been suggested by so good an authority as Beza, who was Calvin's biographer and successor at Geneva, that he was converted through his relative, Olivetan, who urged him to study the Bible. Doubtless there was a truth in all these—that Olivetan and Wolmer influenced him. But his later biographers place his conversion about 1533. That was the year in which the Reformation gained great prominence at Paris, through the patronage of Margaret, the sister of the King. A letter of Calvin's of that date reveals his great interest in the religious discussions then going on. He was then on intimate terms with Roussel, the Evangelical preacher of the Catholics. In November, 1533, there occurred an event which reveals that he had become a Protestant; his friend, Nicholas Cop, the rector of the university, delivered an address, using in it, it is said, the words of Calvin. For this he was charged with Protestantism, because he insisted on justifying faith. So Calvin's conversion was not later than 1533. Calvin speaks of it in one place as sudden, and in another as gradual. His two statements may be harmonized in this way, that after carefully considering Protestantism for a time, he suddenly surrendered himself to God.

IV. *Calvin a Wanderer.*

The address of Cop led to Calvin's threatened arrest, which he avoided by flight. Like Paul, he was let down from a window and escaped, carrying a hoe on his shoulder so as to complete his disguise. Proceedings against him were, however, dropped, and he later returned to Paris. But he did not feel safe there, and so found an asylum at Angouleme, about 250 miles southwest of Paris, with his friend, Louis du Tillet. The fine library of Du Tillet was of great assistance in preparing him to write his "Institutes of Theology." On March 4, 1534, he went back to

Noyon, and resigned all his offices in the Catholic Church. This meant his final break with Catholicism. It is interesting to learn that he was imprisoned there twice "for uproar made in the Church on the eve of Holy Trinity." Whether that "uproar" was his public protest against the papal errors, we do not know, but this imprisonment was the beginning of many persecutions which finally compelled him to leave his native land. He returned to Paris for a short time, and then went to Poitiers.* At Poitiers he revealed his home missionary spirit. For, finding a number of persons who were Reformed, he held religious conferences with them. He then took the next important step after his conversion. In a cave outside of the city he secretly celebrated the Lord's Supper with them. In thus giving the Lord's Supper, Calvin took his place as a minister of the Gospel. He thus shows his missionary spirit here by organizing a congregation.

Then he went to Orleans, where he wrote the preface to his next work on "The Sleep of Souls." It was a work written against the Anabaptists.** This book revealed that Calvin felt he was not only called to be a minister, but a teacher. as in this book he teaches against heresy.

V. *Calvin in Exile.*

But it became too dangerous for him to remain in France. By the end of 1534 the placards against the mass were posted up all over France. This greatly angered the Catholics. So he fled and arrived at Strassburg in Germany at the beginning of 1535. From this time he was

* The order of his stay in these different places, Angouleme, Poitiers and Orleans, seems to be somewhat uncertain.

** The Anabaptists were those in the Reformation who denied infant baptism. Many of them were excellent people, but some were fanatics and heretics. They differed from our Baptists because they did not require immersion as a necessity.

an exile from his native land. He then went to Basle, where he published his famous "Institutes of Theology." This book reveals him as a theological genius. It was the greatest work on dogmatic theology produced during the Reformation, and yet it sprang from the brain of a young man only twenty-six years of age. His preface to it, which is dedicated to the king of France, was a masterpiece of apologetic literature. He dedicated it to the king in the hope that it might lead him to lessen his persecutions against the Protestants. The charge had been made by the Catholics against the Protestants that Protestantism was destructive, not constructive. Calvin replied to this by showing in his "Institutes" that it was constructive. It contained a whole system of theology based, however, on the Bible, and not on the Church, as in Catholicism. But its first edition was briefer than the later editions and was not so sharply Calvinistic on predestination and other doctrines. The work was the completed fruit of his conversion. It gave him great fame among the Protestants of that day.

VI. *Calvin in Italy.*

Calvin, having published his "Institutes," set out on an evangelistic expedition to Italy, to visit Princess Renee of Este, the daughter of the late king of France, but who favored the Reformed. At her palace in Ferrara, he found a circle of kindred spirits. But he was not permitted to stay long, for one of these Protestants, a young singer named Jehanet, at one of the services walked out of the Church as his protest against the adoration of the cross in the mass. The Catholics brought charges against him, which led to an investigation, and the Protestants there were discovered and compelled to flee. Calvin fled to Switzerland. There is a very curious cross at Aosta in northwestern Italy on the border of Switzerland, called "Calvin's Cross." There have been a great many things and places named after Calvin because he visited them during his life, but this is the only one erected to his memory by the Catholics. It seems strange that they would erect this to the memory of the man they hated. It seems that Calvin came to Aosta, which is at the southern end of the great St. Bernard Pass, and there found some secret Protestants. The Catholics learned of his presence and brought charges against him, so he had to flee. And while they guarded the great St. Bernard Pass (famous for its dogs) he, aided by his friends, escaped over the neighboring, but very dangerous pass, named the Col de Fenetre, and arrived safely at Switzerland. The Catholics seemed to have been so glad that they had rid their neighborhood of such a heretic that a few years later they erected this cross. There it stands to-day, and right opposite to it is the Waldensian Church which preaches the Gospel of Calvin.

Calvin went from Switzerland back to France, for the king seemed at that time to be more favorable to Protestants, as he even invited Melancthon to visit his court. He also went back so as to arrange his few business interests that he might leave France and settle in a foreign land. He also brought his brother and sister away with him. Then he started for Germany. But in order to get there he had, on account of a war, to make a long detour southward by way of Lyons and Geneva. He arrived at Geneva in the latter part of July, 1536.

VII. *Farel's Call to Calvin.*

One of the most dramatic scenes in the history of the Reformed Church was Farel's call to Calvin. Calvin came to Geneva expecting to spend a night there. Instead, he spent most of his life there and became the great Reformer of Geneva. Farel, when he heard that Calvin was at Geneva, called at his hotel and begged him to stay. Calvin demurred. He said he was a student and was not made of the stuff to be a Reformer. He declared that he wanted to go to Germany to study. Farel persisted in his appeal, but when he saw that Calvin was not inclined to yield, he reminded him of the punishment that came to Jonah when he ran away from duty. But still Calvin refused. Finally Farel, his mighty spirit rising within him at the sense of the great need of helpers at Geneva, rose from his chair, and laying his hands on Calvin, said with his voice of thunder, "May God curse your studies, if in our great need you do not come to our help." Calvin was awed; he trembled like a leaf; he asked to be permitted to think and pray over the matter until morning. In the morning he surrendered and decided to stay. He thus became Geneva's great Reformer, and made that city, even according to the testimony of so strict a Lutheran as Andrea, the model city of that age.

VIII. *Calvin at Geneva.*

Calvin began his work at Geneva without any salary, but by the following February a small salary was voted to him. He at once began lectures on the Epistles of Paul, but it took Geneva some time to realize what a prize she had gotten in him. He had hardly settled there when in October, 1536, he, together with Farel, went to Lausanne, where Viret was trying to introduce the Gospel. To do this a disputation between Catholics and Protestants was held. At this disputation Calvin gained great fame by the masterly way in which he refuted the doctrine of transsubstantiation from the Church Fathers, so as to completely silence the priests. After his return to Geneva he prepared a Catechism and a Confession of Faith for that city. He also began the more difficult task of preparing its ordinances, so as to make it a Protestant city. But when his very strict laws were attempted to be enforced, the looser element, called the Libertines, reacted against him; and taking advantage of a slight difference between Calvin and the Bernese in regard to Church discipline and the use of bread at the Lord's Supper, they produced a situation that compelled Calvin and Farel to resign, because they refused to administer the communion as ordered. They were dismisesd April 23, 1538.

IX. *Calvin at Strassburg.*

Calvin was invited by Bucer to come to Strassburg as pastor of the French Reformed Church, so as to gather the French into a congregation. He proceeded to organize this congregation just as any home missionary would do to-day. His stay of three years at Strassburg was destined to be of great value to him and the Reformed Church. Thus he was able, in his congregation, to carry out his idea of church government, as he had not been able to do at Geneva. He also began lecturing on the Bible, and it is likely that his "Commentary on Romans" was given there in the form of lectures. Here, too, he rewrote his "Institutes of Theology" into the form in which they now are, though somewhat revised before his death. He made them more sharply Calvinistic, especially on the doctrine of election. At Strassburg, too, he formulated his method of worship, which was mainly a translation of what was used by Bucer, though arranged for Bucer and the Strassburg Church by Diebold Swartz, a minister of Strassburg. In his services he made prominent the use of the psalms and of singing, which Zwingli had not done. Here he was married to Idelette de Bure, by whom he had a son who died soon after birth. But most important during his stay here was his association with the Reformers of Germany, for he learned their viewpoint. Three important Conferences were held at that period to reunite the Catholics and Protestants, at Hagenau, Worms and Ratisbon. In the latter, Calvin took a prominent part. Fortunate was it for Protestantism that he was there, for the yielding Melancthon was apt to concede too much to the Catholics. But the Conferences brought no practical results,.except that in them Melancthon and Calvin, in spite of their differences of character and views, became fast friends for the rest of their lives. His missionary spirit shows itself then in trying to convert the Anabaptists and gain them for the Church.

X. *Calvin Recalled to Geneva.*

Meanwhile affairs at Geneva were going from bad to worse, until the city approached Calvin about coming back. It was, however, a difficult thing to get him to do so after the unkind treatment that he had received. For he had declared to Farel, that he would rather suffer "a hundred other deaths than that cross." But Farel pressed him to return, and finally after months of negotiation, he returned to Geneva, September 13, 1541. He received a salary of about $1000, which was a great relief after his poverty at Strassburg. He now had things his own way, for his friends were in control of the city council. He drew up ordinances which were adopted, and which thoroughly organized the city both religiously and morally. In them appeared the germ of the Presbyterial form of government, in which the laity were represented in the consistory as well as the ministers. The germ of the Presbyterial government is representation—the elders representing the congregation. It also contained the germ of the separation of church and state, for the consistory was granted the power of excommunicating members. This gave to the Church a power that did not belong to the State. .This was in contrast with the Zwinglian form of government, in which the punishment of offenders in the church was given to the state who imprisoned and punished them. We say this was the germ of the separation of church and state, for there was, as yet, no complete separation of the church and state as we have it in America. The beginning of religious liberty in Protestantism was not at Geneva under Calvin, but in the eastern canton of Switzerland, the Grisons, where in 1526, at Ilanz, Catholics and Protestants mutually agreed to respect each other's rights. That was about a century before the Pilgrims claimed to have brought religious liberty to Plymouth Rock. But the Pilgrims, from what source did they get religious liberty? Not from England, their home, for there was none there; but from the Reformed in Holland, from which country they sailed to America. Calvin, in these theocratic regulations, tried to make God the Ruler in Geneva—to make all government but the expression of th Will of God. His ordinances were very severe against dancing, gambling, drunkenness, profanity, and any licentiousness in dress, word or act. The reading of bad books was prohibited. They even went so far as to prescribe the number of dishes to be served at a meal. These things seemed severe, but they made Geneva the model city of Europe.

Gradually, however, the leaders of Calvin's party died off and the dissatisfaction with such strict laws increased, until a considerable party was formed against Calvin. In 1547 a number of his opponents were elected to office. At the election of 1548, the parties were evenly divided. Meanwhile Calvin's life was made very unpleasant. His enemies nicknamed him Cain; they named their dogs after him; placards were posted up criticizing him and ballads were sung ridiculing him. It is true the perpetrators were often punished, but these things made Calvin's life unhappy. Once at the Lord's Supper, when unworthy Libertines were coming forward to take the elements without his permission, Calvin flung his arms around the sacramental vessels as he said: "These hands you may crush, these arms you may lop off; my life you may take; but you shall never force me to give holy things to the profane." Indeed, during these conflicts his life was at times in danger. One night fifty shots were fired before his bed-chamber. On another occasion he met a number of his opponents who were armed. Baring his bosom, he said, "You want to kill me, here is my breast." But his martyr-spirit and courage so awed these opponents that they made no attempt. At the next election, February, 1549, his arch-enemy, Perrin, was elected as first syndic, or head of the government. In the midst of these struggles and trials, his wife died, March 29, 1549. His own health was uncertain, due to his anxieties, and increasing nervous headaches. The two parties continued evenly divided until 1553, when Calvin's opponents gained control.

XI. *Calvin and Servetus.*

It was just at this critical time that there came to Geneva a man whom Calvin looked upon as an arch-heretic, Michael Servetus, a Spaniard by birth. He had published in 1531 a work against the Trinity; as a result he was a wanderer, driven hither and thither. In 1553 he published a work, "The Restitution of Christianity," which was pantheistic and denied the full deity of Jesus. He was condemned at Vienne, France, 1553, but escaped and came to Geneva just when Calvin's opponents were in control. At Calvin's instigation he was arrested. His opponents in the government took hold of the case, hoping by it to discredit Calvin. At the examination Calvin pressed Servetus about his pantheistic ideas, that if God was everything and everything, God, as Servetus said, "then the very floor and benches of the room in which they were, were the substance of God," and Calvin went further and said, "then the devil is, in substance, God." To which Servetus replied, with a laugh, "Do you doubt it?" This reveals the flippant as well as heretical character of Servetus.

The result was that the Council ordered Servetus to be burned alive. Calvin sought a milder form of death, but Servetus was burned, October 27, 1553. The burning of Servetus has prejudiced the world against Calvin. But we believe the odium attached to him is excessive and largely unjust. Of course, in the light of our twentieth century, it cannot be defended, but we must judge Calvin by the sixteenth century and not by the twentieth. It is to be remembered, too, that the law that led to Servetus' condemnation was based on Catholic jurisprudence of the time before Calvin, and in its day heresy was everywhere punished with death. The Catholics had treated it as treason, for they held that the church and state were united, and therefore, heresy to the church was treason to the state, and so punishable with death. This law continued in existence until the seventeenth century. Calvin was not directly responsible for his burning, for the city council that ordered it was led by Calvin's opponents, who had been trying to use the trial against Calvin. And the burning of Servetus was not only due to the law of that day, but to the spirit of the times. All the Reformers approved it, even the mild Melancthon. It must also be remembered that such acts were done by all in that day. The Catholics put Protestants to death for heresy. The Episcopalians in England did the same to the Catholics. The Lutherans did the same to the Anabaptists—indeed, they put one of the Reformed, Crell, the chancellor of Saxony, to death at Dresden near the end of the seventeenth century for his faith. And so here the Reformed did it too. It was due to the spirit of the times. But we do not believe it is right to lay the fault of a whole age on one man, as has been done to Calvin. We regret the event, but the Lutherans and Episcopalians all were also blameworthy. And we believe that if Calvin had lived in the light of this century, he would not have approved it, especially if he had seen that our religious liberty is largely the outgrowth of his work at Geneva.

But after 1553 the tide in the city government began to turn toward Calvin. In 1555 an event occurred that led to the arrest of Perrin and others of his party, on the charge of treason. They were executed. This loss of leaders to his enemies placed Calvin in supreme control of the situation in Geneva, and he held it until his death. This gave him relief from opposition for the rest of his life. It enabled him to complete the work at Geneva. It also gave him liberty to do more for the Church at large. For while Geneva was his abode, his heart was

REFORMED MISSION TO BRAZIL 75

with the Church of Christ everywhere.

XII. *The French Mission in Brazil.**

And now occurs an event in connection with Calvin and his church that has received little attention, but is of great importance in a missionary manual like this. We have seen how the Reformation was a great home missionary revival, as everywhere the Reformers and other Protestants tried to convert souls to their Gospel. We now take up the Reformation work among the heathen. Protestantism had hardly been born before it became missionary. We have already noted how Professor Bibliander, of Zurich, wanted to go as a missionary to the Mohammedans. In 1557 the Church of Geneva founded the first foreign mission of the Protestants in Brazil, one year before the Lutherans founded their first foreign mission in Lapland.

In 1555 a colony of Frenchmen, under Admiral Villegagnon, went from France and located on an island in the harbor of Rio Janeiro, Brazil. Admiral Coligny fostered the expedition and Villegagnon professed to be a Protestant. After they arrived at Rio Janeiro, Villegagnon wrote back to Calvin to send ministers. The letter came to Geneva when Calvin was away at Frankford, Germany; but Calvin's missionary spirit had permeated his church and they took action in his absence. They appointed two ministers to go to Brazil, Peter Richer and William Chartier. These, together with a number of Genevese, went out with the next expedition from France and arrived in Brazil March 9, 1557. Among the Genevese were several young men who were sent out to be especially trained for missionary work among the natives, among them De-Lery, a student of theology, who afterwards wrote the history of the expedition and described their efforts to preach to the natives.

* See Good, "History of the Reformed Church in the United States," pages 3-11.

After they had arrived at Brazil, Villegagnon was at first very friendly and supported their religious services, but soon he began to criticise and then to quarrel with them, especially about the Lord's Supper. The truth was that the Catholics had sent an emissary in the last expedition, who was winning Villegagnon back to Catholicism. Finally matters came to an open breach between Villegagnon and the ministers, so Chartier returned to France to get the judgment of the churches on the matters in controversy. Meanwhile the quarrel became so great that the Genevese, with Richer, left the island on which Villegagnon had his fort and went to the mainland to live among the natives, where DeLery and the other young men, who were to be missionaries, were already living. The natives gladly received them. DeLery and the others tried to preach to the natives, but accomplished little because their stay was so short. Nevertheless it was the first attempt to reach the heathen by the Protestants. Soon after this, Richer and his party went back to France; so the missionary effort ended. On their return to France they were in the greatest danger. The vessel proved unseaworthy; fire threatened them, and starvation came on them, until just before they came in sight of France, they were about to draw lots as to who should be killed for food. A few years later Villegagnon returned to France and spent the rest of his life in bitter controversy against Calvin and the Protestants.

We have said that this was the first Protestant foreign mission. It also gave the first martyrs for Protestant missions. For when the vessel, on which Richer and the rest were returning, had been out at sea a few days, the captain offered a boat to any who were afraid to continue the voyage on account of the danger. Five of them went in the boat to land, and lived at first with the natives. Four of them found their way back to Villegagnon, but he arrested them as spies and put three of them to death. One of them, John Boles, did not return to Villegagnon, but continued living with the natives. He preached Protestantism to them with such power and influence that the Jesuits finally became alarmed at his success. They had him arrested and put to death. Thus the Reformed were the first to establish Protestant missions and also to have the first missionary martyrs for Protestantism.

XIII. *Calvin's Last Years.*

Calvin, in 1559, was able to complete the school system of Geneva by founding the Theological Academy, out of which has grown the present university of Geneva. The building, which was opened June 5, 1559, is still used as a theological school, and has over its door the motto in Latin, "After darkness, light." To this school came students from every Protestant land, and it became a great educational centre. It completed Calvin's ideal of a Christian commonwealth, for to pure preaching and morals was added religious education. But after 1558 his health declined. On February 2, 1564, he delivered his last lecture in the Academy, and he was carried to the April communion in a chair. On April 27th the council of Geneva went in a body to his bedside to express their sympathy and appreciation for his great service to the city. He expressed his gratification at their coming and exhorted them to be faithful to their city. The next day the ministers of Geneva came in a body. He spoke briefly to them in a reminiscent way, and yet his address reveals great humility, and a great desire to exalt God. He died on Saturday evening, May 27, 1564. He left a request that no monument should be erected to his memory, but there is in the cemetery at Geneva a plain stone with the letters "J. C." marked on it, which, it is said, marks his grave. But though no monument was then erected there, his monument is the Reformed Church that he organized, whose members are now found in every part of the world. The Reformed and Presbyterian churches, now numbering about thirty millions, are his direct descendants; in fact, all the other Protestant churches, except the Lutheran, are indirectly the result of his work.

XIV. *Calvin's Theology.*
This is a large subject, of which only the briefest outline can be given here. He held to

1. *The Supremacy of Scripture.* The Bible was the infallible and sufficient rule of faith and duty. Where does Scripture get its authority? The Romanists said, "From the Church." "No," said Calvin, from "the testimony of the Holy Spirit." This was the self-evidencing power of the Bible to us,—the appeal that its truths made to us, for we feel the Holy Spirit speaking to us through it as through no other book. This, however, differs from the modern view which makes the authority of Scripture depend on our religious experience of it. Calvin made its authority depend on the Bible itself as objective to us, but proving itself by its own appeal to us. Not our answer to Scripture (as according to the modern view), but Scripture's appeal to us gives it its authority.

2. *Predestination.* This was the eternal decree of God, by which he determined in himself the destiny of every man; in his plan Christ died for the elect. Not all of the Reformed fully accepted Calvin's views, though some seem to go higher than he. Historically, there have been three kinds of Calvinism—supralapsarianism, infralapsarianism, and sublapsarianism. It has been a question to which of the first two Calvin belonged, and his successor, Beza, and the scholastic Calvinists went higher than he. Infralapsarianism is now held by what we know as the Federal school. But many Calvinists have held to sublapsarianism, which is a lower form. Zwingli, Bullinger and Lasco held to it. According to it, Christ died not only for the elect, but for all men. It emphasizes redemption in Christ rather than God's eternal decree, and election is redemptive not metaphysical.

3. *The Lord's Supper.* Here Calvin occupied a middle

ground between the memorial view and the Lutheran. Over against the Lutheran he denied the bodily presence of Christ at the Lord's table—Christ's body, he held, was in heaven. On the other hand he held that the Lord's Supper was more than a memorial—that there was a real presence of Christ in it, but a spiritual one. Hence, his view of the Lord's Supper has been called the spiritual view. He also emphasized the subjective and refused to give objective efficacy to the bread and wine. Faith was necessary in order for sacramental efficacy. This subjectivity is shown in most of the Calvinistic liturgies, which require us by faith to lift our minds from the bread and wine up to heaven where Christ is, and thus commune with him through the Holy Spirit, who unites Him and us.

XV. *Calvin's Missionary Work.*

Calvin was a city missionary as truly as any city missionary, who to-day is laboring to save any of our cities. He stands out as the typical city reformer, both in morals and religion. Would that we had some Calvin to clean up our cities of New York, Philadelphia and other cities of our land, instead of the superficial, non-religious reformers we have to-day. But Calvin was also a foreign missionary; that is, laboring to save other lands. This he did through his enormous correspondence, much of which is soul-saving in its aim. This correspondence extended all over Europe. What has come down to us fills ten quarto volumes. The number of letters from, to and about Calvin numbers 4,271, and they are directed to no less than 307 persons and organizations. Many of these letters were intended to aid in introducing the Evangeilcal Gospel into new places or to new persons, or else to guide those who were doing missionary work. How anxious do his letters reveal him about the evangelization of England and Scotland and Poland. To aid this evangelization he dedicated some of his works to the crowned heads of

Europe, hoping to make them more favorable to the Gospel. Indeed, sometimes he was too aggressive here, and he would dedicate books to those, to whom this would prove dangerous. Thus he dedicated one of his Commentaries to Elector Frederick III of the Palatine, who, though a Lutheran, he heard was inclining to be friendly to the Reformed. Fortunately for Frederick, he never read the book or his case at the Diet of Augsburg, 1566, about the Heidelberg Catechism would have gone against him. But this reveals Calvin's earnest spirit in spreading the Reformed faith.

So died at the age of fifty-five of overwork, one of the most remarkable men of history. He had his faults, and no one was more conscious of them than himself. But he had tremendous faith in God and he did everything from the standpoint of obedience to God's will. His motto, "My bleeding heart I yield to thee quickly and entirely," deserves to be the motto of every one of his followers.

QUESTIONS

What position does Calvin hold among the Reformers?
In what four things did Calvin excel as a Reformer?
Where was he born and when?
To what position was he appointed as a boy?
Describe his education.
Why did he change from studying for the priesthood to the law?
How did his legal education help him afterwards as a Reformer?
Before his conversion, what was he?
When and how was he converted?
What did he do at Angouleme and Poitiers?
When did he leave France and why?
Where did he go to?
What were his "Institutes of Theology"?
Describe his visit in Italy?

QUESTIONS

What occurred at Aosta?
What was Farel's call to him to become the Reformer of Geneva?
What changes did he make at Geneva?
What caused his departure from Geneva?
Where did he go to?
What did he do at Strassburg?
What effect did his stay at Strassburg have upon him?
What great Lutheran Reformer did he meet in Germany?
Why was he recalled to Geneva?
What rules did he lay down for the city?
Where was there the first religious liberty in the Reformation?
Where did the Pilgrims, who came over in the Mayflower, get their ideas of religious liberty?
What opposition rose against Calvin at Geneva?
What other trials came to him then?
What dangers came to him in Geneva?
Who was Servetus?
Who tried and put Servetus to death?
What mitigates our judgment of the burning of Servetus?
How did Calvin again gain control of the city?
Where were the first Reformed foreign missionaries sent and when?
Who led the expedition, and who were the first two missionaries?
How did Villegagnon at first treat them?
What efforts were made to evangelize the natives?
Describe their journey back to France.
Describe the first martyrdoms for Protestantism and the Reformed?
What school did Calvin found at Geneva?
Describe his death.
Where is his monument found?
Describe his character.

CHAPTER V

THE COMPLETION OF THE REFORMATION IN FRENCH SWITZERLAND BY VIRET AND BEZA AND THE REFORMATION IN HOLLAND

I. *Viret's Birth and Education.*

Peter Viret was the *Boy-Preacher* of the Reformation, for he began preaching at the age of twenty. He was, therefore, the youngest of the Reformers. Although he stands behind Farel and Calvin in importance, yet he did an important work. The three, Farel, Calvin, and Viret, stand together as the great trio of French Reformers. Farel was the Reformer of Neuchatel, Calvin, of Geneva, and Viret, of Lausanne, the city so beautifully located in the northwestern corner of the Lake of Geneva.

The little town of Orbe, in which Viret was born in 1511, is picturesquely situated in southwestern Switzerland. At the age of sixteen he went to Paris to study, and remained there several years. He came home to find the Reformation entering there. The story of its introduction into Orbe is quite dramatic. In Lent, 1531, a friar came to the little town and noisily offered indulgences for sale. One day as he was hawking his wares at the public fountain, which still stands in the center of the town, he was interrupted by a pale man with a stentorian voice asking him the question, "Have you an indulgence for a person who has killed his father and mother?" The monk was confounded. At this the questioner, who was none other than Farel, stepped to the curb of the fountain and began preaching the Gospel. His eloquence was so great that the people left the indulgence-monger, and gathered round the new preacher. As a result of Farel's preaching,

two leading men of the town were converted. The result of this sermon was excitement enough to please Farel, but he deemed it best to go away. Later Farel came back to Orbe, and on Palm Sunday, 1531, he entered the large church there, followed by a crowd, and went up into the pulpit, where he preached. The Catholics in the congregation tried to howl him down; "It was a glorious noise," said a Catholic, "you really could not have heard it thunder." Then they proceeded to pull Farel out of the pulpit, but the Bernese magistrate protected him and led him safely out of the church. The next Sunday Farel, by order of the Bernese, preached again in the church at Orbe, and had the first Protestant audience, ten persons in all, among them Viret. On May 6, 1531, young Viret, after having been ordained by Farel, preached his first sermon as pastor of the church, at the age of twenty. And on Whitsunday of that year, Farel administered the first Protestant communion to eight persons.

II. *Viret as Farel's Helper.*

Farel went away, leaving the infant church at Orbe in the care of Viret. Under his care it increased tenfold in a year, so that by Easter, 1532, he had seventy-seven communicants. His missionary spirit led him to go to the neighboring town of Payerne in September, 1532. There he challenged a priest, who had publicly defended justification by works, to a debate, and the day was appointed for it. But before it took place the priest met him on the street and beat him so severely that he left him almost lifeless. After his recovery, he went with Farel to Geneva in 1533. These two men, Farel and Viret, so different in nature, complemented each other; Farel so aggressive and headstrong, Viret so mild in manner and sweet in his preaching. Yet Farel loved Viret as a son and Viret looked up to Farel as a spiritual father. At Geneva the Catholics attempted to poison the Reformers, but Viret was the only one who ate of the poisoned soup. Fortunately the remedies promptly administered saved his life.

But the thin face of Viret, as it has come down to us in his portraits, reveals that he was never a well man afterwards. After his recovery he aided Farel there in preaching. He then went to Neuchatel as pastor for a short time, but on his way back to Geneva was held up by a providence. He met the Bernese army and Bern sent him to Lausanne (which Bern had recently captured from the Duke of Savoy), in order to reform the city.

III. *Viret at Lausanne.*

He became the great foreign missionary to Lausanne and the district of Vaud, which had not yet received the Protestant Gospel. He had as unpromising a field as our missionaries to-day to Catholic lands, Spain or Brazil. Farel had been driven out by the Catholics at Lausanne, what hope was there for him? He at first preached in the streets and at his hotel. Finally to further the Protestant cause, a great disputation was held at Lausanne, October 1, 1536. Farel and Calvin, with other foreign ministers, were present to help Viret. Farel placed ten theses before the conference for debate. Viret led in the discussion, assisted by Farel and Calvin. When the debate on transubstantiation took place, a monk arose and publicly disavowed Catholicism. Another dramatic episode occurred in the debate on justification. Farel called for the reading of the verse in the third chapter of Romans, "We see how that it is freely, without desert, without the deeds of the law, that man is justified." At this the Catholic disputant, Dr. Blancherose, burst out, "I do not believe that that is there." A Bible was brought to him from the neighboring Franciscan Convent, and he was bidden to read it for himself. Scarcely believing his eyes, he cried out, "It is true." His conversion completed the victory for the Reformed.

Viret labored not only in Lausanne, but all over the district of Vaud, so as to convert it to Protestantism. But his greatest work was the founding of an Academy at

Lausanne in 1537 for the training of ministers. This was more than twenty years before Calvin was able to found a similar school at Geneva. He labored quietly for many years as professor and lecturer in that Academy. Then he came into conflict with Bern, which ruled Lausanne, on the question of church discipline, and as he refused to obey the authorities at Bern, he was deposed and left in 1559.

He then went to Geneva, where he was elected pastor. His sermons gave great satisfaction, for he was one of the most remarkable orators of the Reformation. His preaching was sweet, yet forceful, so that it held the audience with rare power. Calvin was the nervous orator, Viret the persuasive one. Calvin carried his audience by the forcefulness of thought and logic; Viret by his sweetness and persuasiveness.

IV. *Viret in France.*

But after being in Geneva for two years, in 1561, he became pastor at Nismes in southern France, where he was very successful. Then he became pastor at Lyons for a short time. But his position was very difficult, for the first civil war of the Huguenots with the Catholics had broken out. In 1566 he was driven out of Lyons, and in 1567 he was called by the Huguenot Queen of Navarre, Jeanne D'Albret,* to come to Orthez as pastor and professor. But in 1569 the Catholic troops burst into this district of Bearn, captured Orthez, Pau, and other places, and drove away the professors. Viret was captured and imprisoned at Orthez. The Huguenot army came to his relief and captured the chateau of Chevany, where he was imprisoned, and set him free. On August 23, 1569, the Queen of Navarre made her triumphal entry into Pau, her capital. But the anxieties, sufferings, and labors proved

* For her interesting life, see Good, "Famous Women of the Reformed Church," pages 71-80.

too great for the man who had not been strong since he was poisoned at Geneva, and he died at Orthez, 1571.

So died the one who had begun, almost as a boy, to preach the Gospel. He was of stronger mind than he has been given credit for by historians. He wrote several strong theological works, as "Christian Instruction." Among the Reformers he was the ironical one. What Erasmus used before the Reformation, and Voltaire, two centuries after it, he used to some extent; namely, satire against the Catholics. In this he was the forerunner of Agrippa D'Aubigne, the greatest satirist of his day and a Huguenot.* Only recently has the ability and influence of Viret begun to be realized in connection with the 400th anniversary of his birth.

V. *Beza—Introductory.*

Theodore Beza was the *Gentleman* of the Reformation. Not that the other Reformers of the Reformation were not gentlemen, but Beza excelled them all. The French are proverbially polite, but Beza was the quintessence of French politeness. He was above all a *Christian Courtier*, for in his early life he had been trained in the French court; and later, to the graces of the courtier he added those of the Christian. Of all the Reformers, he was the one best fitted to state and defend Protestantism before the King and Queen of France at the famous Colloquy of Poissy, 1561. He was not only the Christian gentleman, but also one of the most learned scholars of his day. And he was also the last of the Reformers, living more than a quarter of a century after the others had passed away. If Erasmus, the famous scholar who published the New Testament in Greek, may be said to have begun the Reformation, Beza, who, as a great scholar, also published the New Testament, may be said to have closed it.

* For his life, see Good, "History of the Reformed Church in Switzerland," pages 116-121.

VI. *Beza's Birth and Education.*

Beza was born at Vezelay, France, June 24, 1519. He was a puny child, and lost his mother when he was quite young. He had a wealthy uncle who reared him in his own home. One day when he was nine years old, a member of the king's council was the guest of his uncle, and noticing young Theodore, said he was about sending his nephew of the same age to school at Orleans to a Professor Wolmar. So Beza's uncle sent Theodore with this man's son, and thus Wolmar, who ten years before had taught Calvin, was now the teacher of the boy who was later to become Calvin's successor. Under him Beza gained such a command of Latin and Greek, as few men of his day possessed. But better than that, Wolmar influenced him to the Bible, and thus prepared him for Protestantism. Wolmar taught Beza for seven years at Orleans and Bourges; and when he went back to Germany, so great was his love for Beza that he wanted to take him with him. But Beza's father refused, so Beza remained at home to enter the study of law. In 1539, having finished the university, he went to Paris to practice law. But law did not interest him, so he led the life of a scholar rather than of a lawyer. And as he had plenty of money (for his uncle had died) he became a gentleman of leisure. Poetry attracted him and he wrote his "Juvenalia," in imitation of the classics.

VII. *Beza's Conversion.*

But the influence of Wolmar ever remained with him. During these years his ideal (which had been prevented by his father), viz., to go to Germany to be with Wolmar, still hung before his eyes. How remarkable is the lasting influence of a good teacher. The high ideals of Wolmar remained in his mind, and kept him from becoming what was so common among Frenchmen of means and culture— a man of loose morals. Wolmar was to Beza what Wyttenbach was to Zwingli. Then God's providence came in to help. His older brother died and that sobered him. Then came a serious illness, so severe that his life was for a time despaired of, and so long that it gave him time for deep thought. As he remembered his worldliness and sinful condition, he came to deep conviction of sin, and out of that he came to forgiveness, and Wolmar's Savior became his. Knowing that France was no place for a Protestant, he suddenly fled to Geneva, where he arrived October 24, 1548.

VIII. *Beza at Lausanne and Geneva.*

The first thing Beza did was to fulfill the ideal of years —to go and visit Wolmar in Germany. On his return to Geneva, he happened to stop at Lausanne, where Viret was just founding the Academy. Viret felt that Beza was the man he needed, and so Beza became professor of Greek, and taught there for nine years. In 1558 he resigned at Lausanne after a brilliant career, in which the number of students had grown from a mere handful to 700. He left for the same reason as Viret, because he approved of the use of church discipline by the Church, which Bern opposed.

In Geneva he became Calvin's assistant; for Calvin's work had grown far beyond his failing strength. When Calvin opened his academy at Geneva in 1559, Beza became its first rector or head. For this his splendid knowledge of the classics and his high position in literature amply fitted him.

IX. *Beza at Poissy.*

In 1561 occurred the greatest event in Beza's life, and one of the most dramatic in the history of the Reformation, the Colloquy at Poissy, near Paris. This reveals Beza's missionary zeal, for he wanted to convert the court of France to Protestantism in the hope that France would follow. What a contrast! Thirteen years before he had left France for exile, and now it was the king who invited him to return. For the king of France was willing to give

Protestantism a hearing. The Protestants of France looked around for a man who could measure up to such an occasion. Calvin could have done it, but he was too sickly to leave Geneva; and besides, he had so many enemies in France that it would have been dangerous. So Beza was chosen, and no one was better fitted by grace, eloquence, and learning than he. One of the most beautiful suburbs of Paris is St. Germain, with its magnificent forest. There the King of France had his palace. Near it, about three miles away, in a nun's convent, the famous Colloquy took place, September 9, 1561.

No more magnificent assembly could have been present. There was the boy King, Charles IX, his mother, later the infamous Catherine de 'Medici, and all the nobles of the court in all their brilliant costumes. There were also the great dignitaries of the Catholic Church in their most gorgeous robes. And there stood Beza, the Christian courtier, the best apologist of the Protestants. As Beza reached the rail before the gathered court, he and his colleagues knelt on the floor and prayed aloud the beautiful Huguenot "Confession of Sin." Its beauty made a profound impression. And then with wonderful eloquence, grace, and great ability, he summarized before the Catholic court the faith of the Protestants. He was listened to respectfully until he came to speak about the Lord's Supper, until he happened to say that "the body of Christ is as far removed from the Lord's Supper as the heavens are from the earth." The Catholic prelates broke out with the exclamation "he has blasphemed," and for a few moments there was much confusion. But the queen-mother commanded silence. Having finished his address he presented to the King a copy of the Confession of the Huguenot Church, the "Gallic Confession." Then occurred another sensation. The leader of the Catholics, Cardinal Tournon, asked that Beza's words be not accepted, at least until a day had been appointed in which they could be answered. The queen-mother said, "We are here to hear both sides. Reply to the address of Mr. Beza."

But the Cardinal was afraid to answer Beza, and so the famous Colloquy closed. Never perhaps in the history of Protestantism was such a magnificent defense made before so magnificent a court. Beza remained in France for a year and a half, counseling the Huguenots in their first civil war. This Colloquy made him the acknowledged head of the French Church. Then he returned to Geneva and after Calvin's death in 1564, he became the head, also, of the Church in Geneva.

X. *His Last Years.*

Just before his death there occurred the Escalade. The Duke of Savoy, to whom Geneva had formerly belonged, had always been anxious to recover the city for himself. This would have meant the extinction of Protestantism there. So the Genevese were always on the alert against Savoy. But on the night of December 12, 1602, one of the longest and darkest nights of the year, eight thousand of the Duke's soldiers secretly approached Geneva. The advance guard put ladders to the walls so as to scale them. They were encouraged by the Jesuits, who whispered, "Climb bolder, each round is a step heavenward." They had scaled the walls to the number of two hundred; they had already gotten so far as to approach the inside of one of the gates, which a traitor had promised to open to them, when a sentinel saw them and discharged his gun. This signal woke up the Genevese and they rushed armed into the streets by thousands. The Savoyards were driven back to the ramparts. But before they got there, one of the Genevese fired a cannon, which, by the hand of providence, was so guided in the darkness that it hit all their ladders and destroyed them. The result was, that as the Savoy soldiers could not escape on their ladders, they were caught like rats in a trap. Many were killed and those captured were beheaded as a warning to Savoy. As soon as the conflict was over, the people streamed to the Reformed cathedral, where Beza held a thanksgiving service. The 124th Psalm, translated by Beza, was sung, and every year since, on that day, a commemorátive service is held in Geneva, and that Psalm is sung.

But Beza was now an old man. He lived longer than any of the Reformers, even to the great age of 86. On October 13, 1605, he passed away. His last words were significant: "Is the city in full safety and quiet?" Having received an affirmative answer, he sank down and in a few moments passed away as his friends prayed by his bedside. So died the last of the Reformers, a scholar and a theologian, a statesman and a poet. But Beza lives in the hearts of the French to-day more by his metrical translation of the Psalms than by anything else, for the singing of these Psalms has been the great power in the Huguenot Church.

XI. *Brave Little Holland.*

Brave little Holland, the land of one hundred thousand martyrs of our faith! The land, that had fought the sea and conquered it, had also to fight the Roman See and build dykes against its floods of superstitions, heresies, and cruelties. A peculiarity of the Reformation in Holland was that it had no one commanding Reformer, who rises above the others as does Luther in Germany, or as Zwingli and Calvin do in Switzerland. It was a people's Reformation, a mighty popular uprising against popery. There were many Reformers, brave and noble men and women, but no one of them towers far above the rest. Its history is not, therefore, so picturesque because it cannot be gathered around one great personage. Only two characters have become at all prominent, Guy de Bres, the author of the Belgic Confession, and Prince William of Orange, that magnificent statesman; only he was a politician rather than a religious reformer. We will try and use these two men as clues to the Reformation in the Netherlands.*

* It will be noticed that in speaking of the Reformation, we include Belgium in the Netherlands, though they are now separated: for Belgium was at that time included with

XII. *The Early Reformation.*

The Reformation in the Netherlands passed through three periods, Lutheran, Anabaptist, and Reformed. The first influences for Protestantism came into Holland from Germany. Luther's writings came in very early. The Reformation appeared first in Belgium. Jacob Spreng, the provost of the Augustinian monastery at Antwerp, preached the Evangelical Gospel, it is said, as early as 1517. He was arrested and condemned, but recanted. Broken-hearted at his weakness, when set free, he preached the Evangelical doctrines more than ever. Threatened with arrest again, he fled to Germany. Henry of Zutphen, another monk of the same cloister as Spreng, having heard Spreng preach the Evangelical doctrines, fled to Luther at Wittenberg and returned to Antwerp, where he preached with such power that the Church of the Augustinians could not hold the people. He was the great preacher of his age. Antwerp hung on his lips. He was arrested and imprisoned and expected to give up his life for his faith. But a great crowd of his friends broke into the prison and set him free. The enmity of the Catholics was so great that the monastery that produced Spreng and Zutphen was razed to the ground in 1522. Still, however, the preaching continued. Great crowds went wherever there was Protestant preaching in spite of the fact that such preaching was forbidden by law. In 1523 two Augustinian monks, Voes and Esch, were publicly burned at the stake in Brussels as adherents of Luther. As the fires were kindled, they repeated the Apostles' Creed, sang the TeDeum and prayed in the flames, "Jesus thou Son of David, have mercy on us."

Meanwhile the gospel was entering Holland as well as Belgium. On September 15, 1525, a Protestant martyrdom occurred in front of the Prince's palace at the Hague. John

Holland in the Netherlands. And the Reformation appeared in both, though Belgium later became almost entirely Catholic.

Van Bakker, a young Hollander, had been preaching the Evangelical Gospel and had been to Wittenberg. He returned but retired from the priesthood and was a farmer, though still preaching. He went back to the priesthood and was then arrested, tried, condemned and martyred. They tore his priest's robes from him, and he replied: "In the dress of a citizen, I look more like a Christian than before." Before he died, he called to his brethren, "Be of good cheer. As valiant soldiers and stimulated by my example, defend the truth of the gospel against all detractors." After him the list of martyrs became so great that it is impossible to describe them or to give their noble dying testimonies. It is said that during the reign of Emperor Charles V there were already fifty thousand martyrs in the Netherlands.

XIII. *The Netherlands Become Calvinistic.*

Protestantism in the Netherlands was, as we have said, at first Lutheran. Then Anabaptism seemed to gain the ascendency. Finally, however, the Netherlands became Reformed. This was due to the fact that a number of Calvin's pupils came into Belgium, where as Frenchmen, they were welcomed by the people who also spoke French, Calvin's language. From Belgium the influence of Calvinism spread north to Holland. The severe doctrines of Calvin seemed especially to appeal to the Dutch mind. The leader in this, if any one can be called a leader, was Guy de Bres, the author of the Belgic Confession or the creed of the Netherlands.

XIV. *Life and Early Preaching of Guy de Bres.*

Guy de Bres was born at Mons about 1522. He came under Protestant influences in his early manhood. In 1550 when the placards were placed in the towns against Protestantism, he fled to England, and joined the Church of the Refugees in London, of which Lasco was the pastor. In 1553 when King Edward VI died and Queen Mary came to the throne, he was compelled to flee. He might have found a refuge in the city of Emden in northwestern Germany. But no, he went back to his own country, though at the risk of his life, because he was so anxious that his family and friends should have the gospel. He became a traveling evangelist and missionary in southwestern Belgium and northeastern France. For two years (1554-1556), he preached at Lille. His missionary zeal led him also to evangelize in its environs. The crown of his work were four martyrs in 1556, who died with the prayer on their lips "Lord Jesus, into thy hand we commend our spirits." That persecution disorganized his work there and he went to Ghent for a short time.

Then he went on his second exile. London had been the place of his first exile; Frankford in Germany was the place of his second, where he probably met Calvin. Indeed, he went farther in order to study, for he went to Lausanne and Geneva. But he could not keep himself from work, for he had the true missionary spirit. When his ruler, Emperor Charles V, died and Philip II became ruler of the Netherlands, back he went to Belgium. He preached at Lille, then at Antwerp and then at Tournai. At Tournai he organized eight congregations. The Protestant movement became so strong there that they had a night demonstration of it, when they sang Psalms in the streets and the public places; yes, even before the priests' houses. Guy had too much common sense to approve of this, for he knew it would cause a reaction, and it did. The government appointed a commission against them and Guy had to leave. He was a veritable "bird of passage," for he dared not stay long in any one place. All this reveals his bravery, for like Damocles he lived with the sword of death continually hanging over his head.

XV. *The Belgic Confession.*

It was while at Tournai that he had written the Belgic Confession. Before that time the Dutch and Belgians had had no creed except that they used several catechisms, as

Calvin's and the Heidelberg. But he felt the need of a common bond for the churches of his land. Another reason why he wrote it was to oppose the Anabaptists, some of whom were heretical. After he had composed it, he sent it to different ministers in his land and abroad, especially to Saravia, professor of theology at Leyden. Saravia sent it to Calvin, who approved of it, but advised that it be set aside for the Gallic Confession which had just been adopted by the Reformed Churches of France in 1559. De Bres followed the advice partially, for it is evident that his Confession was based on the Gallic, which it very much resembles. In 1561 he sent it to the Reformed ministers in Emden, who were Zwinglian, and they approved of it. It was submitted a second time to the ministers at home, and their suggestions were embodied in it. It was approved by the pastors of the Walloon and Flemish Churches, and published in 1562 in French for the south provinces, and in Dutch for the northern provinces.

The history of its official adoption is quite interesting. On October 2, 1565, about twenty nobles met in the city of Brussels. They were led in prayer by Francis Junius. He, when a young man, as pastor at Antwerp, had been so zealous and fearless as to preach when the flames that were consuming a Protestant were reflected on the walls of the room where he preached. These nobles consulted how they could protect themselves from the Spanish yoke. They signed an agreement. And the next year between three and four hundred of them rode into Brussels and presented a petition to the Regent, Margaret, requesting that she remove all restrictions of Protestantism. The reply, says Hansen, to the petition was so equivocal that the people changed the word "moderation" in it to "murderation." Still the appearance of so many nobles gave courage to the Protestants, and they held a synod at Antwerp in May, 1566. This meeting was a secret one, for the danger was great. The members were required to give a countersign,—"the vineyard,"—before they were permitted to enter. This was the synod that formally adopted the Confession of Guy de Bres. At the synod of Dort, 1618, it, together with the Heidelberg Catechism and the Canons of Dort, was adopted as the creed of the Dutch Church.

XVI. *The Later Preaching of Guy de Bres.*

Guy de Bres, having completed his creed, later died for it. All the creeds of the Reformed and Presbyterian Churches have many martyrs, but this was the only one whose author died for it. Guy now went on his third exile. This time he went to Sedan. From Sedan he returned to Antwerp in 1566. He found that by that time the people had largely become Protestant. Great open-air services were being held. Thus in June a Reformed minister, Hermann De Strycker, preached on the outskirts of Ghent to assemblies of seven to eight thousand. On June 28, at eight P. M., six thousand persons assembled near Tournai to hear a Protestant minister, and ten thousand the third day thereafter at Pont a Rieu. De Bres, after remaining at Antwerp for three weeks, went to Valenciennes. Here the Reformation had first appeared in 1561. It showed itself, as it had at Tournai, by the singing of Psalms in the streets. In 1562 two of the Protestants were about to be put to death. Their cry, "Father eternal," caused a tumult. The scaffold was torn down and they were freed. But that only brought severer measures against them. In 1565 a Protestant minister secretly preached there for a year. Just before Guy's arrival this minister had announced a public service, and from two to three thousand attended. When Guy arrived, a dozen services were held, attended by three to six thousand. It is said that three-fourths of the town (which had thirty thousand inhabitants) attended Protestant services. In August the images were torn out of the Catholic churches, and Protestant worship was introduced into them. But then an army was sent against Valenciennes by the Catholics, and it was besieged for seven months. Meanwhile the Catholics outside were busy working on the Catholic party within the walls. As it was evident that it could not hold out, Guy, with four others, fled. They were arrested and imprisoned in the castle at Doornik, then at Tournai, and finally at Valenciennes. He was tried and condemned. From prison he wrote letters to his brethren, to his old mother, his wife and children.

XVII. *Martyrdom of Guy de Bres.*

On May 31, 1567, he was executed at the city hall of Valenciennes. He went to death as to a marriage feast. When he got to the foot of the ladder, he attempted to pray. The executioner did not permit it, but pushed him up the ladder. But on the last round of the ladder he cried to the people, "Be submissive to the magistrates, faithful to the truth." He protested that he had taught nothing but the truth of God.

So died one of the flaming heralds of the truth. But, though dead, he did not die. His Gospel remained to found the Dutch Reformed Church. For as the great successor of Guy de Bres came the great statesman, William of Orange.

XVIII. *Prince William of Orange.*

Just at the time of De Bres' death, the Reformed fled to Germany, and there held two synods, at Wesel (1568) and at Emden (1571), to organize their church. After that they returned to the Netherlands. For the Duke of Alva was sent to the Netherlands to crush out Protestantism by the introduction of the inquisition. But the Dutch would not submit to the inquisition. Prince William of Orange arose in 1568 to defend the liberties of the Netherlands against Spain, and to defend Protestantism against the inquisition. In 1572 there came a thunder-clap out of a clear sky as the "sea-beggars" captured the town of Briel, and William was made stadt-holder or governor. At first in the war with Spain he suffered much from the lack of funds and the smallness of his army. As a result the town of Haarlem was besieged and captured by the Spaniards. The Spaniards tied the Reformed citizens of Haarlem together, two and two, and threw them into the lake of Haarlem. In the face of all these reverses, William of Orange publicly professed the Reformed faith in 1573.

The next year came the siege of Leyden. The inhabitants of that city, knowing they would be massacred by the Spaniards like the citizens of Haarlem, determined to die rather than surrender. They ate the leaves off the trees and the grass in the streets, but they would not surrender. William of Orange came to their rescue with a fleet. The dykes were broken down so that the ocean could come in, and his fleet relieved them, October 3, 1574. The first thing that the thankful people did was to go to the Great Dutch Church there and thank God for their deliverance. And then they founded, as a memorial of their deliverance, the great university of Leyden. In 1576 the different provinces of the Netherlands, south as well as north, Catholic as well as Protestant, united in the pacification of Ghent, which united all the Netherlands against Spain.

XIX. *The Death of William of Orange.*

This great prince, William of Orange, continued his victorious career in war and diplomacy until July 10, 1584, when he was shot by an assassin. The Catholics, having been unable to destroy him by fair means, resorted to foul. His life had often been threatened. The assassin, Gerard, who killed him, pretended to be a Calvinist, and stayed at Delft, where Prince William was living, so as to become familiar with William's habits. As the prince rose from the dining table and passed out of the room, this man, who was in hiding outside of the door, fired at him. The prince realized that his end had come. "My God, take pity on my soul: my God, take pity on this poor people," was his dying cry. His sister asked him if he trusted his soul to Christ, and "Yes" was his last word. He was buried in the New Church at Delft, where a beautiful marble monument has been erected to his memory. But his greatest monument is the Netherlands, which, having been saved by him from Spain and the Catholics, soon became the leading Protestant nation of Europe. William of Orange is, without doubt, one of the greatest characters in history. He had all the qualities of a great world-leader,—far-sightedness, tact, breadth of mind, firmness of purpose, and knowledge of human nature. His absolute self-sacrifice for his country has raised him to be one of the noblest of patriots, and his devotion to our Reformed faith has made him one of the greatest of her sons.

QUESTIONS

What was the significance of Viret among the Reformers?
Describe Farel's visit to Orbe, and its results.
Describe Viret's preaching at Payerne.
Describe the poisoning of Viret.
What was the Conference at Lausanne?
Why had Viret to leave Lausanne, and where did he go?
Describe his labors in France.
What was the significance of Beza among the Reformers?
What was Wolmar's influence over him?
What led to his conversion?
Where did he go, and what did he do?
What did he do later at Geneva?
Describe the Conference at Poissy.
What was the Escalade, and how was it celebrated?
Describe Beza's death and the influence of his Psalms.

HOLLAND

What was the great peculiarity of the Reformation in the Netherlands?

In it what two characters rise into prominence?
Through what three periods did the Reformation in the Netherlands pass?
Describe the early Reformation at Antwerp.
Describe the early Reformation in Holland.
How did it happen that Calvinism at last gained control?
Describe the early life and preaching of Guy De Bres.
Why did he write the Belgic Confession?
Whom did he consult in writing it?
How was it adopted as the creed of the Netherlands?
Describe the later preaching of Guy De Bres.
Describe his martyrdom.
Why did William of Orange become the defender of the Netherlands?
What capture roused the Netherlands to resistance?
Describe the sieges of Haarlem and Leyden.
How was William of Orange assassinated?
What was the character of William of Orange?

HEIDELBERG

CHAPTER VI

THE REFORMED REFORMERS OF GERMANY

I. *Bucer and Strassburg.*

The original Protestant Church in Germany was Lutheran, and that Church is still the largest there. But very soon the Reformed doctrines began to appear. They appeared about the same time at two places, at Emden, in northwestern Germany, and at Strassburg, in southwestern Germany. Strassburg was one of the free cities of Germany, and therefore had greater freedom to receive doctrines from abroad than the imperial cities, where in religion the law was, "like prince, like people." Strassburg lies on a flat plain a few miles west of the Rhine, and its tall cathedral spire can be seen for many miles around. Like that church spire, Strassburg became a finger pointing heavenward, as it exerted a wide influence for Protestantism in western Germany.

II. *His Birth and Youth.*

The Reformer of Strassburg was Bucer. Though around him were gathered several other Reformers, as Zell and Capito, yet he was the leader. He was born at Schlettstadt, in Alsace, November 11, 1491. At the Latin school there he soon showed such precocity that his friends prophesied that he would become pope if he could. But a better sphere was to open up to him,—that of a Reformer. At the age of fifteen he entered the Dominican monastery there. In 1516 he was transferred to Heidelberg, where he could enjoy the advantages of the university. ·At Heidelberg he seems to have come into contact with humanism and to have become a humanist.

III. *His Conversion to Protestantism.*

In 1518 Luther came to Heidelberg on a tour of visitation to his order, and held a disputation. Although Luther belonged to a rival order of monks, the Augustinian, yet

Bucer, though a Dominican, attended the disputation. Luther's address produced a profound impression in southwestern Germany, but on no one did it make more impression than on Bucer. Its truths came like a revelation to him. He was at once won, and a private conference which he then held with Luther deepened the impression already made. Luther, it is said, was so pleased with him that he declared that "Bucer was the only Dominican without guile." But for a Dominican to become a follower of Luther was, at that time, considered a contradiction. The Dominicans not only opposed Luther because he was an Augustinian, but they upheld Tetzel, the seller of indulgences in Germany, whom Luther so bitterly attacked, because he was a Dominican. So Bucer, for his Evangelical leanings, was compelled to leave his order. But where should he go? In the early Reformation it was hard to find an asylum for Protestants. Finally he found a refuge with Count Francis of Sickingen, who was favorable to the Reformation. But, as the Count was soon overthrown by his Catholic enemies, Bucer had to flee, and went to Weissenberg. There he married a nun, being one of the first of the Protestants to marry. For that act the Bishop of Weissenberg excommunicated him, and he fled to Strassburg in May, 1523.

IV. *Bucer at Strassburg.*

When he arrived at Strassburg he found that the Evangelical Gospel had already entered the city. Matthew Zell, the preacher at the cathedral, had, as early as 1521, begun to preach it in the chapel of St. Lawrence in the cathedral. And when that chapel became too small, he preached it in the cathedral. When the Catholic bishop locked the pulpit there against him, the carpenters of a neighboring street made a portable wooden pulpit, which was carried into the cathedral whenever he preached, and carried out when he was done. In 1523 Zell completed the breach with Rome by marrying. His wife, Catharine, was a woman of forceful character.* She made his home a refuge for all persecuted Protestants who came to Strassburg, as Farel and Calvin. Zwingli stayed with her on his way to Marburg. She was also the first female authoress of the Reformed Church, and she proved such a defender of Protestantism that Catholic leaders hesitated to break a lance with her. Zell in the same year (1523) introduced the Protestant Lord's Supper in the cathedral.

Then, after Zell had begun this work, Capito had come to Strassburg from Basle and Mayence, where he had been cathedral preacher. He became pastor of St. Thomas' Church at Strassburg. At Basle he had been in sympathy with Erasmus and Ecolampadius. His great ability is shown in that he possessed a three-fold academic degree of doctor, in medicine, law and theology. Still another Protestant of Strassburg was a prominent layman, Jacob Sturm, who belonged to a family that for more than two centuries had given Strassburg her ablest magistrates. In 1522 Sturm was made mayor of the city, and held it many years afterward. From 1525 to 1552 he was Strassburg's representative in ninety-one political and religious negotiations.

These were the leaders who had labored at Strassburg before Bucer came there. No wonder, therefore, that Bucer declared that Strassburg was ready for an overflowing harvest. Bucer came there to complete the Reformation and become the leader. But at first his work was very much circumscribed, as the city council would not permit him to lecture publicly because he was an excommunicated priest. So he began delivering lectures in Zell's house on the Pastoral Epistles. But he had the missionary spirit, and it was hard to keep him from preaching. A few months later he was permitted by Zell to preach in the St. Lawrence chapel of the cathedral. His services continually increased in popularity. As the bishop refused to permit him to preach

* See Good, "Famous Women of the Reformed Church," pages 45-54.

from the pulpit, Zell loaned him his wooden pulpit. The Catholics tried to stop his preaching. One day, while he was preaching in the cathedral, the monks in the choir of the cathedral began singing their service so as to drown his voice. Bucer's audience murmured at this, and one of them went to the monks and advised them to wait until Bucer was through. But the monks defended their course, and as a result a riot was imminent between the two congregations. Bucer's congregation picked up their seats and foot-stools for use against the insolent monks; when just then the chief magistrate appeared. Both parties were ordered to appear before the city council the next day. The threatened riot brought matters to a crisis favorable to the Protestants; for the city council ordered that nothing but the pure Gospel should be preached.

The next year (1524) completed the Reformation in Strassburg. Bucer was elected pastor of the church of St. Aurelian, and became a great home missionary for the city. This church had St. Aurelian's tomb in it, which was famous for its wonder-working cures, and to which many pilgrimages were made. Bucer preached against all these Romish practices, and also had the wonder-working body of the saint removed. On February 16, 1524, Swartz, Zell's assistant, read the first mass in German instead of Latin, in the St. John's chapel of the cathedral, and on Easter of that year the Lord's Supper was administered after the Protestant fashion in most of the churches.

V. *Bucer's Great Influence.*

Bucer was one of the most important of the Reformers. He emphasized the doctrine of election, not in a metaphysical sense, but as a definition of the "Church," which he said was "composed of the elect," meaning by that, of the saints. He thus emphasized the practical side of election. It is interesting to note that Calvin re-wrote his "Institutes of Theology" here, in which he made election more prominent. Bucer, too, was the first to introduce church discipline and excommunication as the fundamental law of the Reformed Church. We have seen how Calvin followed him in trying to get it introduced into Geneva. The truth was that, before Calvin came, Bucer had come into controversy with Anabaptism, which threatened to become victorious in Strassburg. Bucer gained the victory over the Anabaptists, but felt that they were right on the subject of church discipline, and so he tried to have it introduced into the churches. We have also noted before, that in the matter of worship, Calvin but followed the method laid down in Strassburg. We thus see that in many respects Bucer was one of the most influential of the Reformers.

VI. *Bucer and the Lord's Supper.*

Bucer at first was a whole-souled follower of Luther, but of Luther in his early period, when Luther emphasized the subjective in the Lord's Supper. When, later, Luther began to emphasize the bodily presence of Christ in the Supper, Bucer could not follow him. For he, like Zwingli, had been a humanist, and his mind demanded a view of the Lord's Supper that was not encumbered with so many rational difficulties. He, therefore, inclined to the Zwinglian view. In 1525 Luther was not satisfied with Bucer's statements, and Bucer was charged with departing from Lutheranism on this doctrine. So Bucer went over to the Swiss, and at the Conference at Marburg, 1529, he was rated among the Zwinglians. Luther there pointed his finger at him and said, "You are a knave." At the diet of Augsburg (1530) he was, therefore, not allowed to sign the Augsburg Confession. So he drew up and presented the "Confession of the Four Cities," whose statements on the Supper were Lutheran but could include the Reformed within them.

VII. *Bucer as a Union Man.*

Even before the death of Zwingli, Bucer began to swerve from the Zwinglian view. He became the great mediator between the Lutherans and Zwinglians on this doctrine. After much labor on his part, he finally succeeded

(1536) in getting Luther to agree to a compromise creed called the Wittenberg Concord. Its phraseology on the Lord's Supper was Lutheran, but it could be made to cover the Reformed view also. He then tried to have this creed adopted by the Swiss, but in vain. For they considered that Bucer was juggling with words in his phraseology of the Lord's Supper, instead of being clear and outspoken. The truth was he was no longer truly Reformed, and was so considered by Bullinger and the Swiss, who refused to adopt his Wittenberg Concord.

VIII. *Bucer's Work at Strassburg.*

Bucer tried in every way to build up the Church at Strassburg. The beginnings of a university were made in his day, and John Sturm (who was Reformed), one of the greatest educators of his day, was called to it. He, with Melancthon, were the two most famous teachers in Germany; so that they were called "the two eyes of Germany." But in 1548 the Interim was ordered to be introduced into Strassburg. According to this, various Catholic rites were to be re-introduced into the Protestant churches. Now, while Bucer was yielding toward Protestants, he was firm as a rock against the abuses of Catholicism. He declared "man dares do nothing against conscience and the truth." So he resigned. Fortunately, a call came to him from England, and he went there in 1549. After his departure, Strassburg became high Lutheran. The Reformed were driven out, and for two centuries were not permitted to worship there.

IX. *The Reformation in England.*

England, like the countries on the continent, had begun to feel the movements toward Protestantism. King Henry VIII fell out with the Pope because he could not get a divorce from his queen so that he might marry Anne Boleyn. He, therefore, declared the Church of England independent of the Pope, and made himself the head of it. He suppressed the monasteries because they were so powerful and also so wicked. But, although he broke with the Pope, he was not willing to become a Protestant. Indeed, he persecuted and martyred Protestants. Thus William Tyndale, who had become a Protestant, was compelled to flee. Tyndale, angered in a controversy with a priest, had declared that every plough-boy in England should have a copy of the Scriptures. As it would not have been safe for him to translate and publish them in England, he fled to the continent. There he had the New Testament published and sent back to England in large quantities. The Catholics became so alarmed that they tried to buy up the whole edition. But the money made in this way only enabled the publishers on the continent to publish more copies and send them to England. They were largely sold and secretly read. The Catholics, unable to stop the circulation of his Testament, hunted for Tyndale, and soon were hot on his track. He was finally treacherously arrested at Antwerp, taken to Vilvorde, and there put to death, October 6, 1536. His last words were, "O, Lord, open the King of England's eyes." This prayer was answered, for King Henry VIII began to see that his only safety over against the Pope lay in the Bible, and Coverdale was commissioned to publish a translation. So that by the time of the King's death, the Bible was permitted in England; and, of course, through it Protestantism grew rapidly. In 1547 the King died, and his son, Edward VI, reigned in his stead. He was a Protestant, and with his accession Protestantism came in everywhere. The leaders of the Reformation in England were Cranmer, Archbishop of Canterbury, Ridley, Latimer,* and Hooper.

* The conversion of Latimer is interesting as showing how a Catholic rite can be used to make a Protestant out of a Catholic. Bilney had been converted, and in order to bring the Evangelical Gospel to his friend, Latimer, he made a confession in the confessional to Latimer. When Latimer heard Bilney's story of forgiven sin, he, too, was converted.

X. *Bucer in England.*

But among the Protestants there was a great lack of scholars able to meet the Romanizers in the Anglican Church. So Cranmer invited a number of the Reformers of the continent to come to England. Peter Martyr, Bucer, and Fagius went there. Bucer, with true Evangelistic zeal, was glad to go and convert this distant land to Christ, and when he arrived in England was cordially received by Cranmer and the British Reformers. He was appointed professor of theology at Cambridge, and began lecturing there on January 10, 1550. His lectures were such a rare combination of learning and spirituality that they gave great satisfaction. In the summer of 1550 he was the leader in a disputation at Cambridge, for the Catholics in the Anglican Church were still strong, and they tried to have as many elements of Catholicism remain as possible. About this time the Prayer-book of the Anglican Church was revised, first in 1549, and again in 1552. The first was very unsatisfactory to Protestants because there were so many relics of Catholicism left in the worship. Bucer was asked to pass criticism on it, which he did in a lengthy pamphlet. While he approved of much of it, he yet criticized it for having Catholic elements in it. And its revision of 1552 agrees with a number of his recommendations, although the leading Anglican historians of the Prayer-book deny that his criticism had much to do with these changes. At any rate, the second Prayer-book was nearer the worship of the Reformed.

But it was still far from Reformed worship, as is shown by the later dissatisfaction with it by the Reformed Reformers, Peter Martyr, Calvin, and Bullinger. This dissatisfaction of the Reformed with the Prayer-book was also shown by the fact that two Reformed liturgies were also published in England just at the time that the Prayer-book was published. If the Reformed had been satisfied with the Prayer-book, why did they publish these? They were the liturgies of Poullain and Lasco. Lasco's especially stands out in contrast with the Prayer-book, for he, with Bishop Hooper, was the leader of the Puritan party in England. They wanted less form and more freedom in the church service, and also stricter church discipline than was in the Prayer-book. The Reformed have generally followed Lasco (and also Knox) rather than the Prayer-book, in that free worship became common in the Reformed Churches ultimately.

XI. *Bucer's Death.*

But Bucer did not live long in England,—only two years. Its damp climate did not agree with him. He died March 1, 1551. He was buried with great honor at Cambridge. It is said that not less than three thousand persons took part in the funeral. His body, however, was not allowed to rest in peace, for when Queen Mary came to the throne she ordered the bodies of Bucer and his fellow-Reformer, Fagius, to be disinterred. They were condemned for heresy, and were burned in the market-place at Cambridge, together with their published works. But when Queen Elizabeth succeeded Queen Mary, and the university had again become Protestant, a memorial service was held to Bucer and Fagius. They could not gather up the ashes of their bodies, but they gathered up their teachings and paid tribute to their lives and influence.

XII. *Bucer's Position Among the Reformers.*

Bucer stands out among the Reformers as the Union Reformer—the great representative of Church union. He cared more for union among Protestants than for any of its doctrines. The Reformed criticized him for not being clear in his doctrines, especially on the Lord's Supper. Indeed, Bucer, when he died, was busy on a work on the sacraments against Lasco, who represented the Reformed.* Bucer was ready to sacrifice much for sake of union. He was, therefore, the Broad Churchman of the Reforma-

---

* Harvey, "Bucer in England," page 53.

tion. He was so broad in his theology that he was ready to take all true Protestants in. He is to be admired for his peace-loving disposition, but criticized in that he was so often concessive where he should have been firm. And his theological statements are often double in their meaning, so as to suit both parties. But he exerted an important and peculiar influence in the Reformation on its doctrine, worship and government.

XIII. *Elector Frederick III and the Heidelberg Catechism.*

The Reformed Church was later introduced into another place in Germany than Strassburg. Elector Frederick III, the ruler of the Palatinate, in western Germany, ordered the Heidelberg Catechism (so called because published at Heidelberg) to be written, and it was published at Heidelberg, his capital, in 1563. His surname was Frederick the Pious, because he was a man of great piety. He was an earnest student of the Bible and a man of much prayer. This prince, for the sake of producing peace between the different religious parties in the Church of his land, ordered that this new catechism should be written, and appointed two young theologians of his Church to write it,—Zacharias Ursinus and Casper Olevianus.

XIV. *Ursinus' Birth and Education.*

Ursinus was an east German, born at Breslau, July 18, 1534. He was educated there, having for his pastor the mild and pious Ambrose Moibanus, whose catechism he studied for confirmation, and some elements of which he put into the Heidelberg Catechism, written about fifteen years later. When sixteen years of age, he went to the university of Wittenberg, to sit at Melancthon's feet and became a great admirer of him. The Lutheran Church of Germany was at that time greatly divided between high Lutherans and low Lutherans. Melancthon was the leader of the latter. While Ursinus was studying in the university, he was financially aided by a native of Breslau, one of the leading physicians of Germany, Crato of Crafftheim, who was the private physician to three of the Emperors of Germany. He had entered the university before Ursinus, expecting to become a minister, but had been turned away from it. So he wanted to put some one in his place in the ministry, and aided Ursinus. Money thus invested in the Church is safely and profitably invested. Ursinus amply repaid his kindness by becoming one of the leading theologians of his day. Indeed, he became the spiritual guide of Crato, whom he won to the Reformed faith.

After studying at Wittenberg for seven years, he began traveling. In 1557 he went to the Conference at Worms, where his teacher, Melancthon, had gone as the leader of the Protestants. He then visited Heidelberg, Strassburg, Basle, Lausanne, and then Geneva. Everywhere, because introduced by Melancthon, he was kindly received. At every place he had his eyes open so as to improve himself theologically. At Geneva, Calvin was so pleased with him that he presented him with one of his works. He went to Paris, and on his return stopped at Zurich and learned to know Bullinger and Peter Martyr there. Fries, the professor of Hebrew there, invited him to come to Zurich if he ever needed a refuge. He then returned through Wittenberg to Breslau, his birthplace.

XV. *Ursinus at Breslau.*

He was appointed teacher in the school of the Church in which he had been confirmed, St. Elizabeth's Church. There he taught for two years. But he soon found them years of trouble, for the breach in the Lutheran Church had reached Breslau and had become very bitter. Ursinus, being a follower of Melancthon, was severely attacked by the high Lutherans. The high Lutherans declared that their opponents were not Lutherans, and charged that Ursinus did not teach Lutheran doctrine. They looked with suspicion on Ursinus, not only because he had been a pupil of Melancthon's, and used one of his works as a textbook, but also because he had been traveling in Reformed lands. Ursinus, therefore, published a pamphlet on the sacraments in defense of his views. But his publication only made matters worse. His enemies seized on certain passages in his pamphlet to show that he was Reformed and not Lutheran. The truth seems to be that, although his pamphlet was Melancthonian, yet there were undoubtedly outcroppings of Calvinism in it. In his travels he had unconsciously imbibed some Reformed views. The result of these attacks on him was that he resigned and left Breslau. But where should he go? He said that if Melancthon were living he would have gone to him at Wittenberg, but Melancthon had just died. He went to Wittenberg, where the university professors would have gladly detained him as teacher. But he made up his mind to go to Zurich.

XVI. *Ursinus at Zurich.*

A few days after he arrived at Zurich he wrote a letter which stated that he had come to full agreement with the Reformed. He there studied at the feet of Peter Martyr. He thoroughly reviewed the doctrines of the Bible, especially election, and in the light of the Bible became strongly Reformed in his faith. In 1561 the Elector of the Palatinate called Peter Martyr to be professor of theology at the university of Heidelberg. He, however, declined, but recommended Ursinus. Ursinus accepted, and went to Heidelberg in the summer of 1561. The next year he was appointed to write the Heidelberg Catechism. For such a work he had been prepared by providence. For he had been teaching the young at Breslau. And his experiences there were a special preparation for him. He was, by nature, inclined to be melancholy. And his dismissal from Breslau and separation from his friends there greatly dispirited him. These troubles and disappointments prepared him to write a catechism, whose motto is comfort.

XVII. *Casper Olevianus.*

Olevianus was a west German, born at Treves, August

10, 1536. Treves was one of the sacred cities of the Catholics in Germany, because it was said to contain the holy coat of Christ—the coat which they said He had worn. In this most Catholic city he went to school until the age of fourteen, when he was sent to France to study law. From Paris he went to Orleans and Bourges to study, thus following in the footsteps of Calvin, who had studied in these universities. He seems to have come into contact with the Protestants in France, for an incident decided him to study for the Reformed ministry. One day, while walking along the bank of one of the rivers that flow through Bourges, together with the oldest son of Elector Frederick III of the Palatinate, who was also a student there, several German students of the nobility came in a boat to them and invited them to take a boat-ride. Unfortunately the prince accepted the invitation, and fortunately Olevianus declined. For the students, some of them being under the influence of liquor, began rocking the boat so that it overturned and threw them into the river. Olevianus leaped into the water to save the prince, and almost lost his life in the attempt. While he was thus hanging between life and death, he made a vow that if God would spare his life he would become a minister. God heard his prayer, for a servant of the prince, who came running to the rescue, unable to save his master, saved Olevianus. From that time Olevianus became an earnest student of the Bible. After a brief visit home, he went to Geneva and studied theology under Calvin.

XVIII. *Olevianus at Treves.*

While he was in Switzerland he met Farel, that fiery herald of the Gospel. Farel told him it was his duty to go back to his native city, Treves, and start Protestantism there. So in June, 1559, he returned to Treves to do what might be called foreign missionary work. For Catholic Treves was as foreign to the Gospel as Ecuador to-day. It seemed a foolhardy thing for a young theological student to try to convert so intensely Catholic a city as Treves. It seemed like putting his head into the lion's mouth, and, as we shall see, the jaws of the lion of Rome very nearly closed over him.*

When he returned to Treves he became a teacher; and, finding that there were a number of persons who wanted Protestant preaching, he, on August 10, preached the first Protestant sermon in his school. Forbidden to preach in his school his friends found a small church for him, which soon became so crowded that the people sat on the pulpit steps and put up ladders outside at the windows so as to be able to hear him. But the Catholics became active against him. Charges were preferred against him that, as a layman, he had no right to preach. His adherents replied that, according to the German law of 1555, the Protestants, who adhered to the Augsburg Confession, had the right to worship, which was true. But then the Catholics brought charges that Olevianus was not a Lutheran and an adherent of the Augsburg Confession, but was a Calvinist, because he had studied under Calvin; and Calvinism had no legal standing in Germany. He, however, continued preaching with great power, so that in about a month one-third of the city declared its adherence to Protestantism. He must have been a remarkable preacher for so young a man. Several times he was called before the Electoral council there and forbidden to preach. He, nevertheless, kept on preaching, declaring that he must obey God rather than man.

But by September 16, the Elector who ruled Treves, alarmed at the progress of Protestantism, returned to the city from Augsburg, where he had been attending the German diet. And he brought soldiers with him to enforce the Catholic worship. He sent a Catholic priest to Olevianus' church to steal in and take his place in the pulpit.

*For a fuller description of Olevianus at Treves, see Good, "The Heidelberg Catechism in Its Newest Light," pages 201-241.

The priest came there before Olevianus and went up into the pulpit. But the congregation rose against him, and he was in danger of being mobbed, when Olevianus, who had meanwhile entered the church, led him out in safety. It, however, was becoming very dangerous for Olevianus to preach. One day, after he had been forbidden to preach, he asked the congregation whether they would stand by him if the priests would try to lay hands on him. The reply of the congregation was that they would stand by him "through thick and thin." It became so dangerous for him that he was escorted to and from the church by an armed bodyguard of his friends.

On October 11, Olevianus and the leaders of the Protestants were imprisoned. The charges against them were heresy and conspiracy, both of them high crimes and punishable with death. He and his friends would probably have suffered death had it not been for the intercession of the neighboring Protestant princes. They were finally released by Christmas and exiled, as were all Protestants in Treves. Olevianus went to Heidelberg, where the Elector, who remembered his friendship for his son (who had been drowned at Treves), made him professor of theology and afterward superintendent of his Church in the Palatinate. This experience at Treves prepared him to write the Heidelberg Catechism. If Ursinus had learned the comfort of religion in sorrow so as to write it into the catechism, Olevianus had learned the courage of religion, and he infused it into the catechism. One can understand the martial answer of the catechism to the question, "Why art thou called a Christian?" when we remember his threatened martyrdom at Treves.

XIX. *The Heidelberg Catechism.*

These were the two men appointed by Elector Frederick III to write the Heidelberg Catechism. In spite of their youth (the one was only twenty-eight, and the other only twenty-six years of age), they produced in the catechism a work finer than either of them produced alone,—in fact, one of the finest masterpieces of catechetical literature extant. It is the great experimental catechism of Protestantism. Luther's Smaller Catechism is briefer, but more sacramentarian. Calvin's and the Shorter Westminster Catechism are more intellectual. But the Heidelberg is the great catechism of the heart. This catechism, which was written in 1562, was laid before the synod in January, 1563, and published early in that year. It soon became one of the great creeds of the Reformed Church, rivaled only by the Second Helvetic Confession and the Westminster Confessions. It has been a great missionary catechism, and for this purpose has been translated into nearly thirty languages. It is to-day used in many foreign mission stations, as Japan, China, India, etc.

XX. *Elector Frederick's Defense of the Catechism.*

Elector Frederick was not left at ease with his new Catechism. It was attacked almost immediately by the high Lutherans as tending to Calvinism. Finally the opposition to the Catechism became so great, that in 1566 Elector Frederick III was compelled to publicly defend it before the German diet at Augsburg. So great was the danger to Frederick that his brother urged him not to go to the diet, lest he lose his electorate, and perhaps his life. In fact, while he was at Augsburg, a rumor came to Heidelberg that he had been deposed, yes, beheaded. But Frederick had the martyr spirit. He declared that he was ready to loose everything for his faith, for he believed his catechism to be thoroughly Biblical. So he went to the diet. He arrived a short time after it had opened, and found it packed against him, as the Catholics had joined with the high Lutherans, who were determined that he must give up his catechism or lose his realm. Only one friend among them at all stood up for him, the Elector of Saxony, who, like him, was a low Lutheran. The charge against him was that the only Protestant creed recognized by law in Germany was the Augsburg Confession, and that the Heidelberg Catechism was a Reformed creed and therefore had no legal standing. This was true, for the Reformed had no legal standing in Germany until at the end of the Thirty Years' War (1648), nearly a century later. Remembering these facts—that he stood virtually alone with the whole diet against him, and that the verbiage of the German law was against him (although its application was somewhat indefinite)—we can look with greater wonder and also greater thankfulness at the splendid victory that he gained there.*

The 14th of May, 1566, is a red-letter day in the history of the Heidelberg Catechism; for on that day Frederick, summoned before the diet to answer for his book, made his great defense. The Emperor and the different members of the diet had already decided on his condemnation. It only remained for the diet to give its sanction. He came into the diet chamber, his son, John Casimir, carrying the Bible before him. In his address he declared that, as for Calvinism, he had not read Calvin's works. But he also added that his catechism was entirely in accord with the Bible and with the Augsburg Confession.* If it were not Biblical, he asked the Emperor and the princes to show it to him. And if he were punished, he declared himself willing to suffer. But none of his listeners were ready to take up the controversy with a man so full of the Bible as he was. Moreover, his address, by its sincerity, spirituality and courage, so awed the assembly that, when he ended, the impression he had made was so profound that no one could reply. His solitary friend, the Elector of Saxony,

* For a full description of this defense, see Good, "The Heidelberg Catechism in Its Newest Light," pages 184-200.

* He meant the Altered Augsburg Confession of 1540, whose article on the Lord's Supper had been changed by Melancthon so as to allow room for the Reformed in it. But his opponents argued from the original Augsburg Confession of 1530, which would have excluded the Reformed.

seized the psychological moment and said, "Fritz, you are more pious than all of us." The result was that nothing was done against the Catechism. Its use was permitted in Germany, and as a result we in America are using it to-day. But except for this magnificent defense of Frederick it would have been strangled almost as soon as it was born, and we would have never known its comforts. Elector Frederick went back to Heidelberg from the diet, and was gladly received by his subjects, many of whom looked upon him as one risen from the dead, for they never expected to again see him alive.

XXI. *Ursinus' and Olevianus' Last Years.*

Elector Frederick III continued to rule the Palatinate ten years after he made this defense. He died October 26, 1576. He had been a wise, pious ruler, and under him his land had prospered. Instead of using his money for war, he used it to build up churches, schools and charities. When asked why he built no forts, he replied in the words of Luther's hymn, "A mighty fortress is our God." His great comfort in his last moments was prayer and the reading of the Psalms. "Lord, now lettest thou thy servant depart in peace," was his cry. He will ever be held in lasting remembrance by every one who loves his Catechism.

When he died, a reaction took place in the Palatinate. His son and successor, Lewis, was a high Lutheran. As a result, Lutheranism was reintroduced into the land, and Ursinus and Olevianus were compelled to leave. Ursinus was called to Neustadt, west of Heidelberg, where Count John Casimir, the son of Frederick III, was the possessor of a small county. This prince founded a university at Neustadt, and called Ursinus, together with the other Reformed professors of Heidelberg, to it. It greatly flourished. But Ursinus was overburdened by work and weakened by sickness. His old melancholy came back on him. He complained of his work as a "treadmill." He continued teaching until death gave his weary soul release on March 6, 1583.

Olevianus also left Heidelberg, but was soon called to Herborn, and became a missionary to introduce the Reformed faith into the districts of Nassau, etc., northeast of Heidelberg. There Prince John of Nassau, the brother of William of Orange, started a university and made Olevianus its rector or head. He taught there until his death, March 15, 1587. As he was dying, one of his colleagues, Professor Alsted, asked him whether he felt sure of his salvation. He replied in one Latin word, "Certissimus," which means "most certain." The comfort of the Heidelberg Catechism is crystallized in that one dying word of his, "most certain."

Of these two men, Ursinus and Olevianus, Ursinus was the stronger intellectually, and ranks next to Bullinger and Beza among the second generation of Reformers. Ursinus was rather the teacher, but Olevianus was the missionary— a great home missionary, as superintendent of the Church of the Palatinate. But Elector Frederick III also had the missionary spirit, and whenever he saw an opportunity of introducing the Reformed faith, he was quick to utilize it, especially by sending his beloved Heidelberg Catechism.

QUESTIONS

Describe Strassburg.
What order of monks did Bucer join?
What was the religious situation at Strassburg when he arrived?
Who were the other Reformers there?
Describe his early preaching there.
What attitude did he take on election and church discipline?
What was his early view on the Lord's Supper.
What did Luther say of him at Marburg?
What was the significance of the Wittenberg Concord?
Did the Reformed accept it?

How was Bucer driven out of Strassburg, and where did he go?
Why did England leave Catholicism?
Describe Tyndale's life.
Why was Bucer called to England?
Where did he teach in England?
How did he oppose the Catholic party there in the Anglican Church?
Describe his death and funeral.
What was done to him after his death?
What position does he take among the Reformers?
Who was Elector Frederick III of the Palatinate?
Whom did he order to write the Heidelberg Catechism?
Describe the early life of Ursinus.
How was Ursinus educated?
How did Crato of Crafftheim aid him?
What compelled him to resign at Breslau?
Where did he go?
How did he happen to get to Heidelberg?
How did his previous experience prepare him to write the Heidelberg Catechism?
Describe the early life of Olevianus.
What led him to study for the ministry?
How did he begin at Treves?
What was the effect of his preaching there?
Why did the Catholics object to his preaching?
What did the Elector of Treves do?
How did he escape martyrdom?
How did this prepare him to write the Heidelberg Catechism?
When and where was the Heidelberg Catechism published?
What is its great peculiarity?
Describe Elector Frederick's defense of it.
Describe Ursinus' last years.
Describe Olevianus' last years.

THE TOMB OF WILLIAM OF ORANGE
(See Page 98)

CHAPTER VII

THE REFORMERS OF POLAND, HUNGARY, ITALY AND THE JEWS

POLAND

I. *Lasco's Birth and Education.*

John A'Lasco, the Polish Reformer, stands out as the pure, self-sacrificing Reformer, for he is one of the most beautiful characters among the Reformers. When he was a young man, Erasmus pronounced him "A soul without a stain." He was also a prince-Reformer; that is, he was of princely blood. But he gave up his princedom for Christ, like Moses, "who esteemed the reproach of Christ greater riches than the treasures of Egypt." Though all the Reformers were self-sacrificing, he was more so. His missionary zeal led him to become the Reformer of three lands. Other Reformers reformed one land, as Luther did Germany, and Zwingli, Switzerland. A few reformed two, as Calvin and Beza, who led the Reformation in France and French Switzerland. But Lasco was the Reformer of three lands, Germany, England and Poland. We therefore here come upon one of the most interesting characters among the Reformers.

John A'Lasco (or John of Lask) was born in 1499, in the town of Lask, Poland. His father was of the Polish nobility. From the time he was ten years of age he was reared by his uncle, the Archbishop of Gnesen, one of the highest religious nobles in Poland. In the episcopal palace of this uncle at Cracow he received his education for the priesthood under the uncle's oversight. The archbishop lived in great splendor, and his nephew lived in luxury in the highest society. In 1513 he went with his uncle to Rome, and in 1515 to Bologna to study church law. In 1518 he returned to his native land. There his kind uncle loaded him with honors in the hope that he might, one day, rise to his position of archbishop. Thus, when hardly eighteen years of age, he had the highest hopes placed before his eyes. In 1521 he was ordained as priest, and became dean of Gnesen.

II. *His Travels.*

Lasco loved to travel. In 1523 he started for Italy. On his way he stopped briefly at Zurich, and Zwingli, always a missionary, gave him the first impulse toward Protestantism by inducing him to read the Scriptures. Then he went to Basle. There he got another impulse toward the Reformation by meeting Erasmus. Then he went to Paris, and there the works of Lefevre fell into his hands, and in the court he met Margaret, the king's sister, then leaning toward the Evangelical Gospel. But the memory of Erasmus followed him, so he returned to Basle. There he boarded with Erasmus, who was captivated by this young noble. He thus writes of him, "While a man of no ordinary learning, Lasco is in his life spotlessly pure as fresh-fallen snow, kindly amiable, so that every one begins to live in his society, and all have a sense of bereavement at his departure,—a golden disposition, a true pearl, and so unassuming and free from arrogance, although he is to be called some day to fill one of the highest offices in his native land." Lasco, on his part, became deeply attached to Erasmus, and boasted of being his disciple. Here, too, he met Ecolampadius, for whose piety and learning he had the highest respect, and whose books, especially his expositions of the Scriptures, doubtless brought him to a deeper understanding of the truths of the Bible.

III. *Lasco in Poland.*

When Lasco came back to Poland, after an absence of two and one-half years, he was still only a humanist, like

Erasmus, and for ten years more he remained a Catholic. When he then returned to Poland he found that rumors against him had been circulated,—that he had visited Zwingli and become a heretic, and also that he had married. He was soon able to convince his uncle that these rumors were baseless, but this did not satisfy his opponents in Poland. So he took an oath of purgation, in which he declared that he was still a Romanist and had no thought of separating from the pope. Lasco was still active in supporting the papacy, but his humanism ever came out prominently. He wanted it introduced into the Romish Church, that it might be purified. In 1531 his uncle, the Archbishop of Gnesen, died. The death of his uncle took away from him his strongest support and hope of advancement in the Catholic Church. Still he remained faithful to Rome, and seven years later was made Archdeacon of Warsau. But that was the last honor that Rome gave him.

IV. *Lasco in Exile.*

Soon after (1538) he suddenly quitted Poland, and renounced the Catholic Church. It was evident that during these years humanism no longer satisfied him. He was by nature spiritually-minded, and longed for something better than humanism, especially since he had gradually become convinced that it was impossible to reform the Catholic Church. He did not leave the Romish Church because of pique or disappointed ambition, for he had just received one of its highest positions. He left it because of conviction. But in leaving it and his native land, he made the greatest of sacrifices. He gave up all his splendid hopes of advancement in the Catholic Church. Like Moses, he would "rather suffer affliction with the people of God than to rejoice in the pleasures of sin for a season." But where should he go? All his possessions and hopes were in Poland. He left his native land and everything to go, like Abraham, not knowing whither he went. He could say:

"To me remained no place nor home;
My country is in every clime;
I can be calm and free from care
On every shore, since God is there."

He went to Louvain, in the Netherlands, where he remained three years. There he joined the secret band of Protestants.

V. *Lasco in East Friesland.*

Persecution drove him out of Louvain, and he fled to East Friesland, in the extreme northwestern part of Germany. There, far away from Switzerland, there had already been founded, as early as 1524, a Reformed congregation, the only one in Germany, besides Strassburg. Aportanus, one of the Brethren of the Common Life, to whom we referred in connection with Bullinger, had become Protestant, and preached at the city of Emden, not the Gospel of Luther, but of Zwingli. In 1543 Lasco was appointed the superintendent of churches in Emden, and began his home missionary work very actively and thoroughly. Thus the Franciscan monks still kept up the Catholic service at Emden. The Duchess of Oldenberg, who was the ruler, was timid and feared to silence them. But, just as Knox spoke to Queen Mary so that she trembled, so Lasco bravely addressed his ruler so that she took courage and suppressed the monks. He also thoroughly organized the Church at Emden, reforming it of its evils. He established a coetus,— a weekly Monday meeting, and also a sort of a synod, which looked after the morals of the clergy. In 1548 he went to England to aid in the introduction of the Reformation, and remained there several months. In 1549 he was back at Emden, but, alas, the condition of his Church! The Catholics had triumphed politically in Germany, and the Interim was to be forced on Protestant lands. The seven sacraments and other Catholic rites were to be reintroduced. As the Emden ministers refused to permit this, the church was closed against them. So they held their services in the neighboring graveyard, which was thronged with greater crowds than had come to the church. There, amid the graves of the dead, children were baptized and marriages were performed. Lasco on his return preached in the graveyard. But the Catholic powers learned of his presence, and after he had been there a month he was compelled to leave.

VI. *Lasco in England.*

But where was he to go? He had been driven out of Poland, out of Belgium, and now out of Germany. Fortunately England was opened to him. We have seen in the last chapter how England had accepted Protestantism, and how her King, the pious Edward VI, had called Bucer and Martyr from the continent. There Lasco became the confidential friend of Cranmer, the Archbishop of Canterbury, and lived with him for a time in Lambeth Palace, London. To live in a palace was not new to Lasco, for he had been reared in one in Poland by his uncle. Here he gained a most remarkable influence over Cranmer, and so was led to exert a remarkable influence in England. It seems very probable that it was Lasco's learning and influence that led Cranmer to give up his Lutheran views* and become Reformed. As a result, the Episcopal Church in its creed holds to the Reformed and not the Lutheran doctrines. About the publication of the Prayer-book in 1549, he showed his dissent from it by publishing, about the same time, his own liturgy for the foreign Protestant Church in London, of which he was the superintendent. He aided in the founding of the Puritan or low Church party in the Anglican Church. The fact is that this low Church party was founded by the Anglicans, who had been on the continent and who had sat at the feet of the Reformed Reformers, Bullinger and Calvin. The first of them was Hooper, who was so

* For he was married to a relative of the German Lutheran Reformer, Osiander, and had published in England a translation of a Lutheran catechism.

low-Church that when he was appointed bishop he refused to wear the white robe for his ordination until compelled to. In all these controversies, as against vestments, Lasco stood with Hooper.

But more important was his influence in his own congregation for the further development of the Reformed Church. He became the great missionary to the foreigners in London, and organized them into congregations. No home missionary to-day in London is doing truer missionary work than did Lasco among the Dutch, Germans and Italians then. Strange to say, he was permitted to organize them outside of the Episcopal Church. Nothing but his tremendous influence with Cranmer could have gained this concession, and some of the Anglican Reformers, as Ridley, Bishop of London, objected to it at the time. In his church at Austin Friars, in London, he proceeded to organize the foreigners according to Presbyterial ideas. He organized this congregation in 1550 by the election of elders and deacons. Calvin gets the credit of organizing the Presbyterial Church government, but he must divide this with Lasco. Lasco's London congregation surpassed Calvin's at Geneva in the completeness of its organization. Lasco's Presbyterianism also differed from Calvin's in being democratic, while Calvin's was aristocratic; that is, Lasco gave more power to the people and the congregation; Calvin, more to the upper church court.*

VII. *Protestantism in England.*

But this prosperous congregation of Lasco's in London was not to continue long. Too soon for Protestantism the good King Edward VI died, and Bloody Mary came to the throne. Then followed a reign of terror for Protestantism

* It is interesting to those who belong to the Reformed Churches, rather than the Presbyterian, to know that Lasco's liturgy and church order were closely followed in Holland and at Heidelberg.

in England. Many of the Protestant clergy fled to Germany and Switzerland, and Catholicism was everywhere restored. The climax of these persecutions were the martyrdoms of Hooper, Cranmer, Ridley and Latimer, the heads of the Protestant Church in England, the last three at Oxford (1555-6). Cranmer at first recanted, but his conscience smote him for doing so, and he withdrew his recantation. When he was brought to the stake, he stretched forth the hand that had made the unhappy signature at recantation, held it in the flames until it was consumed, and frequently exclaimed, "That unworthy hand." Fortunately Queen Mary did not live long. When she died (1558), Queen Elizabeth came to the throne and restored Protestantism.

VIII. *Lasco's Flight.*

Lasco did not suffer martyrdom like Cranmer. He and his foreign congregation, 175 in number, were compelled to flee. They sailed from Gravesend, September 17, 1553, singing Lasco's favorite Psalm, the second. But they went out into storm and suffering. They aimed to go to Denmark, where Lasco hoped to gain a favorable reception. On November 8 they landed at Kolding, in Denmark. Lasco went to the Danish court preacher, Noviomagus, stating their sad condition, and begged him to get for them an audience with the King. Before it could be given, they were required to attend church, and the court preacher preached on the pericope of the day, Philippians 3: 7-21. The Scripture passage was full of comfort, but the sermon was full of denunciation of the Reformed because of their view of the Lord's Supper. Lasco then presented the request to the King that they be permitted to remain in Denmark. They were answered five days later that they would be permitted to stay only on condition that they become Lutherans. Now, the Lutherans of Scandinavia are more high church in their ceremonies than the German Lutherans, and they reminded Lasco's congregation of the high church Anglicans, against whom they had contended in England. So his congregation declared that they would rather continue their wanderings than stay and worship with such Romish rites. Lasco then made a second request that they be permitted to stay during the winter and not be driven out to sea in such inclement weather. But they were refused. What to do they knew not. So Lasco went overland to Emden to try and find a place of refuge. Micronius, another of their ministers, went with them in the ship to Copenhagen, where they hoped to find a refuge. At first the Lutheran ministers there received them kindly, but an order from the King of Denmark came ordering them to leave. Their requests, to stay the winter, then to stay a month, then to stay two weeks, were all denied them. They must leave within three days. So away they sailed into the storm and snow. Lasco's two sons had gained permission to remain in Denmark, but this was at the last minute recalled, and they, with their tutor, were compelled to flee to the vessels, which had already started away, by jumping from one ice-floe to another in the harbor. In a few days they arrived in Germany, for the Danish ports were closed against them.

One vessel landed at Warnemunde, where the magistrate received them kindly. But a week after, orders came from Rostock that they must be sent away as they were heretics. They were compelled to travel overland through snow and wind to Wismar, where they met the rest of the refugees. These had found the bay full of floating ice, so that the vessel that landed there stuck fast a mile from the town. During the night a storm arose which drove the ice against the ship, so that the captain wakened the refugees and bade them flee in the darkness over the ice to shore. They refused to do so, as the danger was too great, so they put out to sea, but later landed at Wismar. At first they were permitted to stay there, but the Lutheran preachers heated up the people against them as heretics, and by the end of February they were compelled to leave. Men, women and children, they walked through the storm and snow for many miles to find a place of refuge. The third ship landed at Travemunde, but they were soon driven out as heretics. So the refugees turned to the city of Hamburg, but here the leader of the high Lutherans, Westphal, lived and preached. He it was who had gotten into a controversy with Calvin and stirred up all northern Germany against the Calvinists. On March 24 they were ordered to leave Hamburg. Fortunately they succeeded in getting a ship to take them to Emden, where, after three months of suffering in mid-winter, they at last found an asylum; for Lasco had already come there from Denmark and arranged for their reception. How terrible these sufferings for their faith! Would we be willing to suffer as much for it? And how sad this tale of religious bigotry. Of course, we must remember that those days were not like ours. Times have changed, and the Lutherans of our day would not think of such unkindness. But to the glory of the Reformed be it said that they never cast out suffering refugees in that way. Again and again they received Lutheran refugees and gave them an asylum. Thus when the Lutheran preachers of southern Germany were driven out by the Interim, Bullinger received them gladly and hospitably, even those who had denounced Reformed doctrines; and at Basle, Brenz, the Lutheran Reformer of southern Germany, was cordially received, although he had attacked the Reformed.

IX. *Lasco's Last Days in Poland.*

In April, 1555, Lasco left Emden, as the countess no longer supported him. He went to Frankford, where many refugees from England had already found an asylum. There he met Calvin. The high Lutherans of northern Germany began heating up the Lutherans, who controlled Frankford, against the Reformed. So Lasco visited the neighboring princes, the Duke of Wurtemberg and Elector Otto Henry of Palatinate, to gain their help against the persecutions of the high Lutherans. In this way Lasco came into contact with the Palatinate, which soon after became Reformed.

But a new field was opening to him; his own native land, Poland, was at last receiving the Gospel and calling for him. So he returned to Poland (1556), which he had left many years before. He went back, with true missionary spirit, to become the great Reformer of his native land. Poland needed a great Reformer, for Protestantism there was much divided. Lasco proved equal to the occasion. With great wisdom he guided them. He met with great difficulties, from the Catholics on the one hand, and on the other from the Unitarians, who were beginning to appear. He was active at the synods of 1557 and 1558. He organized their Church along full Presbyterial lines. The minutes of its general synod, which have lately been published, show that it was one of the earliest Reformed synods, even antedating France. He also took an active part in the translation of the Bible into Polish. But he did not live long after his return to his native land,—only four years. He died January 8, 1560. At last, he, whose life had been such a pilgrimage, found rest in the Father's house. At last, he, who gave up all for Christ, received the hundred-fold reward. He had given up a princedom for Christ, but he now received a crown in heaven above.

HUNGARY

X. *Hungary's Reformer, Matthew Devay.*

Devay's real name was Matthew Biroe, of Deva, the name Devay being taken from the place of his birth. While he is the most prominent of the Hungarian Reformers, there are several others who need to be mentioned, as Szegedin and Melius. Hungary was then partly under the Turkish rule and partly under Christian. And the parts that were under Turkish rule had greater religious liberty than those under the Catholic, and there it was that Protestantism spread most widely.

The first Protestantism in Hungary was Lutheranism. Devay studied at the university of Cracow and became a monk. But he felt the influence of the new religious movements around him, and went to Wittenberg, where Luther, seeing great possibilities in him, took him into his own house, and Devay became a great favorite of his. In 1531 he returned to Hungary, determined that the places that knew him as a boy should know the true Gospel. With true missionary zeal, he preached it with great eloquence to both high and low. Soon town after town in upper Hungary, around Buda, followed him into Lutheranism. But the enemies of the Gospel arose and had him imprisoned at Pesth. In prison he converted a blacksmith, who had declared he wanted to share Devay's fate. The king, moved by this, set Devay free.

He then went to Kassa, which, unlike Buda, was under the control of Austria. There the people heard him gladly. But the Catholic authorities had him arrested, and he was imprisoned at Vienna for two years. Bishop Faber, the bitterest foe of Protestantism, tried to win him back to Catholicism. Once when the bishop left the prison, he said, "I would bless thee if thou wert a Christian." Devay replied, "I do not want thy blessing; God blesses me." Released from prison, he went a second time to Wittenberg to tell Luther of the progress that the Reformation was making in Hungary. He returned in 1537 to the Papa district. Here the Catholics bitterly opposed him. About that time Devay changed his views about the Lord's Supper, after reading Calvin's "Institutes." He gave up the Lutheran view for the Reformed. Over no defection from Lutheranism did Luther mourn so much as over that of Devay. He died about 1545, at Debreczin.

XI. *Szegedin.*

After Devay came Stephen Kiss, of Szegedin. He is generally known to English readers, as was Devay, by the name of the town of his birth, Szegedin. Devay had been the bold, eloquent preacher; Szegedin was the learned professor and author. A graduate of the universities of Vienna and Cracow, he, like Devay, went at first to Luther, at Wittenberg, in 1543; though later he, too, became Reformed. On his return to Hungary, Petrovics, the count of Temesvar, appointed him as teacher in his school there. Protected by this prince, he taught and preached the Gospel with large results. But when the town came under the control of King Ferdinand, he, with other ministers, had to flee. There was a providence in this. Had he stayed, he would later have been slain in the terrible slaughter there by the Turks. Driven from place to place by the Catholics, he finally went to Turkish Hungary. His enemies, however, accused him before the Turkish pasha, who imprisoned and scourged him. His sufferings there secured for him great sympathy. His friends at Buda tried to have him released, but gained only the concession that he was allowed to work in his room, bound by chains. He was finally released, 1563, and went to Raczkeve, where he became superintendent over thirty-five congregations under Turkish rule. He died (1572) leaving a large Reformed systematic theology or "Common Places," for he was a learned theologian. He wrote against the Unitarians, who were beginning to appear in Transylvania. Beza called him "A champion worthy of eternal remembrance."

XII. *Melius.*

A third Reformer came to complete the Reformation of Hungary for the Reformed,—Melius. He, too, had gone to Wittenberg to study (1555-1558) under Luther. On his return he was called as pastor to Debreczin, and helped to found what is at present one of the largest Reformed congregations in the world. Though he had, at first, been friendly to Luther, he, like the other Hungarians mentioned above, went over to the Reformed (1559). He wrote the first Reformed Confession, 1562. He died in 1572. He did great missionary work among the princes of Transylvania, so that a number of them joined the Reformed. He strongly opposed the Unitarians. The publication of the Lutheran creed, the Formula of Concord, with its condemnation of the Reformed, led many mild Lutherans in Hungary to become Reformed. In 1567 the first Reformed synod adopted the Second Helvetic Confession. The Reformed type of doctrine seems to have been better suited to the Hungarian type of mind, or it would not have been so generally and quickly adopted by them. Its doctrine of the supremacy of God, and its more rational view about the Lord's Supper, seems to have appealed to the Hungarians, who were, originally, a Semitic race, and combined mysticism with rationality in religion. By the close of the sixteenth century the Reformation had become so general that there were only three of the nobles of Hungary who remained Catholic, and the great majority of the Protestants there to-day belong to the Reformed Church.

ITALY

XIII. *Ochino and Vergerius.*

A Reformation in Italy,—can it be possible that there was a Reformation in the land where the pope ruled supreme? There certainly was one needed, for it used to be a proverb, "The nearer Rome, the worse Christian." Yes, the Reformation broke out even in Italy, and gained a strong hold for a time at several places, at Naples and Lucca. But it was soon cut short by the introduction of the inquisition. In this Italian Reformation, three Reformers were prominent,—Ochino, Vergerius, and Peter Martyr.

Ochino, the Capuchin monk, was the most eloquent preacher in Italy. The Emperor, Charles V, was wont to say that his sermons could draw tears from stones. When he preached his Lenten sermons, the cathedrals at Florence and Naples were filled to overflowing. But he became too Evangelical and had to flee.

But the Reformation struck higher than this monk.

One of the Roman Catholic bishops was Peter Paul Vergerius, who had been sent by the Pope to convert the Protestants. But, lo, he turned Protestant. As he was compelled to flee from Italy for his Evangelical opinions, he stopped at the village of Pontresina, in the canton of the Grisons, in southeastern Switzerland. The priest of the village had just died, and the simple-hearted mountaineers begged him to stay and be their priest. He replied, "You may not like my preaching." They declared that they would be fully satisfied with it. And soon his preaching began to bear fruit as their eyes were opened to the errors of Romanism. They finally decided to put away their images in their church. But what to do with them they did not know. Some of them wanted to sell them to the churches down the valley below them, which still remained Catholic. But others said, "What is wrong for us is wrong for them." And so they were divided. They finally took the images out of their church and threw them into the little mountain stream that flows through Pontresina. And that was the end of Catholicism in that valley for more than three centuries. His missionary zeal there converted that whole valley and also the whole Romansch race. Vergerius went to Switzerland and Wurtemberg, where he died, 1565.

XIV. *The Conversion of Peter Martyr.*

But the ablest of the Italian Reformers and the one of greatest interest to us was Peter Martyr Vermigli, generally called Peter Martyr. For he became identified with the Reformed, and, next to Calvin, was the strongest dogmatician among the early Reformed. He was born in September, 1500, at Florence. This city, which had burned Savonarola, the Reformer, before the Reformation, in 1498, saw the birth, two years later, of one of its sons who was to be the successor of Savonarola in attacking the papacy. Martyr's mother was a woman of deep piety, and poured into him her spirit of devotion. At the public schools of

Florence he was noted for the strength of his intellect and the power of his memory, but above all by a thirst for learning that would stop at nothing. His father wanted him to be educated for civil affairs, and had great ambitions for him there. But the boy disappointed his father by choosing to become a monk and entering the monastery at Fiesole, a suburb of Florence. He first studied philosophy for eight years. It was his intense desire for study that ultimately led him to become a Protestant, because he always wanted to get at the root of things. Thus he was not satisfied with studying Aristotle in the Latin. He learned the Greek, so as to read Aristotle in the language in which he spoke. He did not then know that the learning of the Greek of Aristotle would prepare him to read the Greek of the New Testament, which would open his eyes to the falsity of Rome. He studied so diligently that at the age of twenty-six he had gained the title of "Doctor of Divinity," and his eloquence led him to be placed on the list of preachers for his Order. He preached with great power in a number of the Italian cities.

Providence led him to be appointed a few years later as prior of the monastery at Naples. There is an old proverb referring to the great beauty of the bay of Naples, "See Naples and die." But Peter Martyr saw Naples and lived;—he gained life,—eternal life. He saw something more than its natural beauties, as he there began to see the beauties of divine grace. There it was that he met the first Reformer of Italy, Jean Valdes, a Spaniard. This Reformer was wont to hold spiritual seances in a villa at Chiaja, one of the western suburbs of Naples. Valdes' delightful discoveries in God's Word led a number of prominent Italians to become Evangelical; Martyr was one of them. Soon in his sermons on I Corinthians (which Martyr preached with marvelous eloquence at Naples) it began to be whispered that he was Evangelical. His sermons raised a great storm at Naples, and he was forbidden to preach. But he had influence with the pope, and so the prohibition was removed. When Valdes died, he was appointed prior of the monastery at Lucca. There, too, he preached with great power, and it was owing to his preaching that there were more Protestants at Lucca than in any other city in Italy. But his enemies were watching him, and finally he was summoned to appear before the council of his Order at Genoa. With the summons came a warning that if he obeyed he would be convicted and put to death. So there was nothing left for him but flight. At Florence he met Ochino, like himself in great danger. They determined to flee to Switzerland, but by different roads.

Thus the Reformation was crushed out of Italy. Poor Italy! For three centuries no Protestant Gospel was allowed and she was in darkness. But in 1848 the kingdom of Piedmont gave recognition to the Waldenses. And in 1870, when Victor Emmanuel captured Rome, the Gospel entered with his army. To-day the Waldenses and other religious bodies, notably the Methodists, are bravely trying to conquer Italy from the pope to Christ.

XV. *Peter Martyr's Later Life.*

Peter Martyr, when he left Italy, went to Strassburg, in Germany, where for five years he was professor in the university. He wrote back to his friends at Lucca his great joy in being in a land of Gospel freedom, where he could teach the whole truth without fear of persecution. In 1547 Protestantism was oppressed in southern Germany by the introduction of the Interim. Both Bucer and himself were compelled to leave and go to England, which at that time was in great need of men of learning to support and defend the new Protestant faith. While there he labored with great missionary zeal to convert England to Protestantism. There, while Bucer became professor of theology at Cambridge, Martyr became professor of theology at Oxford university. He found that the Romanizing elements in the Church of England were still strong, so strong as to incite a riot, and in one of them he was in danger of loosing his life. When the danger was over, the young King of England, Edward VI, gave him an audience, warmly congratulated him on his escape, and promised him promotion. At Oxford even bishops attended his lectures, and he saw much of Latimer and Ridley, who, later, with Cranmer, suffered martyrdom (March 21, 1556) for their faith, under Queen Mary, at Oxford. When Bloody Mary came to the throne he was compelled to flee. After a perilous voyage he landed at Antwerp, in the middle of the night. He went to Strassburg, but found that the high Lutherans had forced out the Reformed there. So he went to Zurich, where he became professor of Hebrew. The only prominent event in the later part of his life was his attendance at the Colloquy at Poissy in France, where he ably seconded Beza in his missionary effort to convert the court of France. He died at Zurich, November 12, 1562, deeply loved and greatly regretted. He was an eloquent preacher as well as an able theologian.

THE JEWS

XVI. *The Jewish Reformer.*

One other kind of a Reformer remains, and one whose significance has been little noticed. An attempt was made at missions to God's ancient people, the Jews. It is true, not much was accomplished, but a beginning was attempted. Protestantism had hardly begun to live before she began to do missionary work. We have seen her beginning in Brazil in 1557, in a previous chapter. Now we notice a Reformer who, like Paul, could say, "Brethren, my heart's desire and prayer to God for Israel is that they might be saved."* This man was himself a converted Jew, for Protestantism very early made an appeal, not only to Catholics, but also to Jews. His name was Immanuel Tremellius. He was born at Ferrara, and early came into contact with a friend of

* Romans 10: 1.

Peter Martyr. Baptized a Christian, he soon became teacher of Hebrew in the cloister school at Lucca, which Peter Martyr had founded. Having been a Jew, he had learned their sacred language, the Hebrew; but while teaching Hebrew he also learned what Protestantism was. And he learned, too, what suffering Protestantism brought. For, like his master, Peter Martyr, he was soon compelled by the inquisition to flee. He went to Strassburg, and there taught with Peter Martyr, and then went with him to England, where he taught Hebrew in the university of Cambridge. Driven out of England by the Marian persecution, he fled to the continent, and sought a place to teach in different cities, but without success. Finally he was called as tutor to the children of one of the lesser princes of Germany, the Duke of Zweibrücken. When the Lutheranism of his prince was stirred up, Tremellius was imprisoned for several months because he was Reformed.

He was then called, in 1561, to Heidelberg. There he was made professor of Hebrew and the Old Testament, and held his place for fifteen years. During this time he revisited England, which had again become Protestant under Queen Elizabeth. He was received there with great honor, and was called to a professorship, but declined. His prince, Elector Frederick III, of the Palatinate, appreciated his work at Heidelberg so highly that when Calvin called him as professor for his new theological school at Geneva, he refused to let him go. When Lutheranism was reintroduced into Heidelberg, at the death of Elector Frederick III, of the Palatinate, he was again banished, and became professor of Hebrew in the Reformed Theological Seminary at Sedan, in France. There he died, October 9, 1580. His greatest work was a Latin translation of the Bible, made while he was professor at Heidelberg. But more interesting to us are his repeated efforts to prepare books so that the Jews might learn to know Christ. He tried to lead the Jews to Jesus, the Jews' Savior. Thus he translated Calvin's catechism into Hebrew. And he also translated the Heidelberg Catechism into Hebrew for this purpose. He stands out among the Reformed Reformers as the great Jewish convert and professor. He, in the Reformation, revealed that holy intensity of zeal peculiar to converted Jews (as Edersheim, the author of the best Life of Christ in English), as they try in every way to bring their race to the knowledge of Christ as their Messiah. Tremellius may well be called the father of Protestant missions to the Jews.

QUESTIONS

POLAND

What was Erasmus' opinion of Lasco?
Where was Lasco born?
By whom was he reared in boyhood?
How did he come into contact with the Reformed in his travels?
What rumors were against him on his return to Poland?
Why did he leave Poland?
What sacrifices did he make in doing so?
What work did he perform in East Friesland?
When he returned from England, in what condition did he find the Reformed Church at East Friesland?
What was his great influence on Cranmer?
What were his relations to Hooper and the Puritans?
Describe the Presbyterial organization of his London congregation.
What English martyrs were there in Queen Mary's reign?
Where did Lasco and his congregation flee to?
What was their reception by the King of Denmark?
What was their treatment at Copenhagen?

How were they treated at Warnemunde, Wismar and Travemunde?
Why were they so persecuted?
Where did they finally find an asylum?
What did Lasco do at Frankford?
What were his labors in Poland?

HUNGARY

Who were the three Reformers of Hungary?
What great Reformer did Devay first visit?
When he returned home, how was he persecuted?
What led him to become Reformed?
Describe Szegedin's early preaching.
In what respects did he differ from Devay as a Reformer?
Describe Melius and how did he aid the Reformed?
Why did the Reformed doctrines take among the Hungarians better than the Lutheran?
How widely did the Reformation spread in Hungary?

ITALY

Name the three great Reformers of Italy.
Describe Ochino's life and preaching.
Describe Vergerius' life and preaching.
Describe Peter Martyr's early life and education.
What led him to become a Protestant?
Why did he leave Italy?
After leaving Italy, where did he go?
Describe his life in England.
Describe his life after leaving England.

THE JEWS

Who among the Reformers was the Father of Jewish Missions?
How did he become a Protestant.
Where did he teach?
What did he do for the salvation of the Jews?

KNOX AND MARY, QUEEN OF SCOTS
From an Engraving in the Presbyterian Historical Society

CHAPTER VIII
THE REFORMERS OF SCOTLAND—HAMILTON, WISHART AND KNOX

I. *Hamilton's Youth and Education.*

Patrick Hamilton was one of the two prince-reformers, Lasco being the other. His father was Sir Patrick Hamilton and his mother was of royal blood. He stands out as one of the most beautiful characters of the Reformation. He was Scotland's first Reformer. He was also Scotland's first Protestant martyr, and of all Scottish martyrs, Hamilton is the most attractive.

He was born about 1504 at Glasgow or Linlithgow. Of his youth and education nothing is known. But having the best blood of Scotland in his veins, he grew up to become one of the most accomplished and heroic of her sons. About 1517 he attended the university in Paris where he took the degree of Master of Arts in 1520. There he first came into contact with humanism and with what was better than humanism, namely, Evangelical faith. For Luther's works were beginning to be circulated in France. And when the university of Paris condemned Luther's writings, Melancthon's splendid reply was published and republished there, so great was the demand for it. From Paris, Hamilton seems to have gone to Louvain where Erasmus was living. Then he returned to Scotland and entered the university of St. Andrews in 1523. He not only studied there but also composed a mass (for he was a fine musician) which was sung in the cathedral.

He seems to have been gradually coming more and more toward Protestantism. As a humanist he seems to have especially disliked the monks because of their hypocrisy. And though appointed Abbot of Ferne, he never went into residence as a monk in his own abbey. Instead of becoming a monk he became a priest. His historian, Frith, says "he took upon him priesthood, so that he might be permitted to preach the Word of God." He still, however, had no idea of breaking with the Church. Just then Luther's works began to come to Scotland, and the Scotch Parliament in July 1525 forbade the circulation of Luther's works. The next year Hamilton began to openly declare his adherence to Evangelical doctrines. Early in 1527 Cardinal Beaton, the head of the Catholic Church, began to make inquiries about Hamilton's heterodoxy, and then proceeded to accuse him. Hamilton was in great peril, for Beaton had introduced the inquisition. Suddenly Hamilton found himself confronted with the alternative of dying for his doctrine or publicly recanting it. So he fled to the continent of Europe in the spring of 1527.

II. *Hamilton an Exile.*

He went to Luther at Wittenberg but did not stay long. For the plague broke up the university and compelled its transference to Jena. Hamilton did not follow it there but went to Marburg, where one of the leading German Protestant princes, Landgrave Phillip of Hesse, had just opened a new university. Before that time all the universities had had the sanction of the pope, but this was the first Protestant university opened without asking the pope for his sanction. Hamilton enrolled himself as one of its first students. The Reformer of Hesse had been Lambert of Avignon, who conceived for this young disciple the warmest affection. Lambert thus speaks to the Landgrave about him, "This young scion of the illustrious family of the Hamiltons, which is closely allied by ties of blood to the King of Scotland, who although hardly twenty-three years of age, brings to the study of Scripture a very sound judgment and who has a vast store of knowledge, is come from the end of the world to be more fully established in God's truth. I have hardly ever met a man, who expresses himself with so much spirituality on the Word of God."

While at Marburg he took part in a public disputation. The Landgrave felt himself specially honored at having a prince from such a distant country defend his theses. They were summed up in these two topics, "Christ is the author of redemption and faith is the eye that sees him." They were published and are the only work that has come down to us from his pen. They were really a brief outline of theology and were named after him "Patrick's Places".*

It was the first work on Protestant theology in English. The reading of this booklet led a number in Scotland to become Protestants and some of them to become martyrs for their faith.

III. *Hamilton's Return to Scotland.*

But he had hardly begun his studies at Marburg when he felt called upon to end them. He felt that Scotland was calling him over the sea. His native land needed the gospel. He could not resist the call. He went home to become the first Protestant missionary to Scotland. In the autumn of 1527, after being a little more than six months on the continent, he returned to his native land. It was a heroic return. He must have felt that to return must mean death. But he feared not death. So out of his love for Scotland and for his Savior, he went home to die. He went first to his own family at Kincavil and told them of the blessed peace he had found in the sacrifice of Christ. But his missionary zeal did not permit him to limit himself to his family. He soon began preaching to the people around his home and great crowds came to hear him, for his preaching was so sweet and beautiful. He then grew bolder and preached in St. Michiels at Linlithgow. Listening to his preaching was a young maiden who accepted it. He had given up all ideas of monastic celibacy and so married her at the beginning of 1528.

IV. *Hamilton at St. Andrew's.*

But the arch-enemy of Protestantism in Scotland, Cardinal Beaton, was watching him. He did not, however, dare send armed men to take him. "For such a Protestant

---

*Commonplaces being the name for works on theology in that day.

missionary with royal blood in his veins, and the Hamilton clan at his back, made Hamilton a more formidable heretic than Luther would have been", says his biographer, Lorimer. So the Cardinal resorted to strategy and perfidy. He sent young Hamilton an invitation to come to St. Andrew's for a conference on religion. The simplehearted Reformer walked into the net, though not unconsciously, for he predicted that he had not long to live. But he had the courage of a martyr. He went there in January, 1528. The conference was conciliatory, and he was given freedom to preach. But all this was part of the plot, for he had listeners who took down what he said and later became witnesses against him. An old student friend, Alesius, who was now very prominent as a Catholic, and who had desired to break a lance with Luther, went to him, confident that he would convert him back to Catholicism. But lo, instead of converting the Protestant heretic, he was himself converted to Protestantism. For nearly a month Hamilton disputed in the university on the necessity of a reformation in the Church. He reasoned with them as he had done in his "Patrick's Places," with all the logical power of Thomas Aquinas, but with logic guided by Protestantism. Like Paul, he reasoned with them out of the Scripture. His teaching and preaching became so popular that the Cardinal determined to strike. He was cited to appear at the archbishop's palace to answer charges of heresy. His friends urged him to flee from the country. But he had returned to Scotland to lay down his life for it, if necessary, that thereby Christ might be glorified; and to turn his back now would lay a stumbling-block in the paths of those who were inclined to Protestantism. His brother, hearing of his danger, came with an armed force to deliver him. But a freshet had caused the Forth river to rise, and he could not cross it to save Patrick.

V. *Hamilton's Death.*

Hamilton appeared before the Cardinal's court, and the charges against him were read. He replied to them.

HAMILTON'S MARTYRDOM

A few days later it was publicly announced that he would be sentenced in the cathedral on the last day of February. His house was surrounded by soldiers at night. When the governor of the castle opened the door, he said, "Here am I." They took him away and threw him into the dungeon, shaped like a bottle, in the castle, and about twenty-five feet deep.* On the day appointed, he was brought to the cathedral. He there defended himself so that he silenced his enemies. He was condemned and led forth to the gateway of St. Salvator's College. While they were piling up the wood for his pyre, he calmly took his last meal, and then inquired of the governor of the castle, "Is all ready?" The governor, whose heart was breaking to see such innocence and nobleness put to a cruel death, could only reply, "God give you a better fate." Joyous he went to the pyre. There he prayed for a few moments. The bishop asked him to recant. "No," was the reply; "better that my body should burn in your flames than that my soul should burn in hell for having denied Him." Later he added, "In the name of Jesus, I give up my body to the fire and commit my soul into the hands of the Father." The chain around his body became red-hot and had almost burned him in two. One of the bystanders called out, "If thou still holdest true the doctrine for which thou diest, make us a sign." Two fingers of his hand had been consumed, but he raised the other three. In the midst of the tumult he was heard to cry, "O, God, how long shall darkness cover thy realm." But his arm began to fall. "Lord Jesus, receive my spirit," he was heard to say. His head drooped, his body sank, and his form was reduced to ashes. And on that spot where he died can to-day be found the stone on which are his initials, "P. H.," to mark the place of his burning.

His death made a profound impression. In distant Germany, his friend, Lambert of Avignon, speaking of his

---

* This dungeon is still there.

life and death, said to his prince, "Such is the flower of surpassing sweetness, yea, the ripe fruit which your university produced at its beginning. You founded this school that from it might go forth intrepid confessors of Christ. See you have one such already." But it was in Scotland that the most profound impression was made. "The reek of Hamilton infected as many as it blew upon," was the saying in Scotland. His high rank as a noble, the beauty of his character, his youthfulness (he was only twenty-four when he died), all combined to impress his native land. His death startled the minds of men into attention, so that they asked the question why a young nobleman so gifted and good had been put to death. The Catholics hoped to strangle the Reformation in its cradle by burning him, but, says Lorimer, "it proved an infant Hercules, and strangled the serpents that sought to destroy it." His pyre lighted a light in Scotland that never went out until Knox in 1560 completed the Reformation. His father had died as a hero of chivalry; the son died as a hero for Christ. If Ireland had its St. Patrick to save it from heathenism, Scotland had its St. Patrick in Hamilton the saint to save it from Romanism.

VI. *Wishart's Preaching.*

Sixteen years after Hamilton's death another Reformer appeared in his footsteps, for then George Wishart returned from England to Scotland. Born about 1513, he, in 1538, had at Montrose gotten hold of a Greek New Testament, which he read with several young men whom he was educating. And it read itself into his heart. Cited to appear for heresy before the Catholic bishop, he had left Scotland for England, where he studied at Cambridge for six years. About 1544 he returned to Scotland with great missionary zeal. At Montrose and Dundee he preached the Word of God. His fame had preceded him, and many came to hear him, for since Hamilton's time Protestantism had more and more crept into Scotland. While he was preaching at Dundee, the priests, alarmed, got an influential magistrate to rise up while Wishart was finishing his discourse, and in the name of the authorities forbid him to preach. So he left Dundee and went west to Ayrshire, later the home of Robert Burns, the poet. As the Church of Ayr was closed against him, he preached at the market cross to a larger audience than the bishop, who locked him out of the Church, had. Kept out of the Church at Mauchline, he climbed a dike and preached for three hours. Then he heard that the plague had broken out in Dundee, and he hastened back there. As those who were in health were within the city, and those sick were without, he took his station at the east gate of the town, the Cowgate, and preached to both the well and the sick. While preaching there an armed priest waited at the foot of the steps to assassinate him. Wishart noticed it, seized the priest's hand, and snatched the weapon from him. The crowd rushed on the man to punish him. Wishart saved him by throwing his arms around him and saying, "Whoso troubles him, troubles me."

When the plague ceased he went to Montrose, and while there Cardinal Beaton tried to trick him into captivity. He sent Wishart a letter purporting to have been written by a sick friend who wanted him to come and see him. So Wishart started. Sixty armed men lay in wait for him behind a hill. When he came to the other side of the hill, he suddenly stopped and declared he would go no farther. When asked why he acted so, he replied, "I am forbidden of God; I am assured there is treason." Pointing to the hill, he sent some of his friends thither, who ran back to tell him of his danger. So he escaped, but it was not for long. Soon after he set out for Edinburgh. On the way he stopped at a house. Two of his friends watched him as he went into the garden of the house after midnight. They heard him sighing and groaning, and just as day dawned they saw him fall on his knees and for an hour pray with bitter tears. In the morning they asked him for the meaning of this strange procedure. At first he evaded their question, but finally confessed it was because of his approaching death. That garden had been his Gethsemane, where, like his Lord, he wrestled in prayer. He, however, added, "This realm will be illuminated with the light of Christ's Evangel."

VII. *Wishart's Death.*

After preaching in various places, he finally came to Haddington, where he stayed one night at the country-seat of the Lord of Ormiston. That night the house was surrounded by armed men. The Lord of Ormiston refused to give him up. But the Catholics got the most powerful noble of that part of the country, the Earl of Bothwell, to come and give his word that Wishart would not be harmed. So Wishart was carried away to the Earl's Castle. But the Cardinal bought off the Earl with money, and so Wishart was given over to Cardinal Beaton, who put him in the same bottle-dungeon in the castle of St. Andrew's where Hamilton had been imprisoned. Then he was called before the cardinal's court and charged with heresy. He ably replied, but was ordered to be burned on the next day. As they refused him the Lord's Supper, because he was a heretic, he celebrated it at breakfast with the governor of the castle. On March 1, 1546, just west of the castle, but several blocks away from where Hamilton had been burned, he was put to death. Before his death he said, "I fear not. But I know surely that my soul shall sup with my Savior Christ this night." The hangman fell on his knees before him and begged his forgiveness. Wishart kissed him as a token of his forgiveness. There is a tradition that, as the fire gathered around him, the governor of the castle cried out, "Take courage." He replied, "This fire torments my body, but in no way abates my spirit." Then, catching sight of Cardinal Beaton at a window of a house, he uttered a prophecy, "He who from that high place feedeth his eyes on my torment, within a few days shall be hanged, but at the same window"—a prophecy which came true three months later, as some of Beaton's enemies, together with Wishart's friends, secretly entered his castle, murdered him, and threw his body out of that very window. Thus Wishart, like Elijah, went up to heaven in a chariot of fire. God took the workmen, but continued their work. The blood of the martyrs is the seed of the Church. Hamilton and Wishart, like Abel, being dead, yet continued to speak, as more witnesses of the faith rose (and some were put to death), until Knox came. Scotland has been bought with Christ's blood and also with the blood of such martyrs as Hamilton and Wishart.

VIII. *Knox's Birth and Conversion.*

A man holding a sword before him, whose point rests on the ground,—such is the statue of Zwingli, the Reformer, in the city of Zurich. A man holding a two-handed sword before him,—so John Knox enters history. Thus the first Reformer, Zwingli, and one of the last of the Reformers, Knox, appear alike. Knox, like Calvin, belonged to the second generation of the Reformers, and completed what Hamilton and Wishart had begun. He was a Reformer of many lands, more perhaps than any other of the Reformers, for he labored in England, France, Germany and Switzerland as well as in Scotland. He was a great missionary force wherever he went.

Knox first appears prominently as the bearer of the two-handed sword, which he carried before George Wishart as his guard. Almost nothing is known of his previous life. He was born probably in 1515, at or near Haddington. He studied at the university of Glasgow. Then for many years we hear nothing of him. Thomas William, the Regent's Chaplain, was Knox's earliest instructor in Evangelical doctrine. Of his conversion we know nothing, except that just before he died, he told his wife that it was on the seventeenth chapter of John that his soul first cast anchor. Then Wishart, in one of his preaching tours, came to the noble family of Ormiston, where Knox was tutor. It was in this house that Wishart, as we have seen, was arrested. Knox wanted to accompany him. But Wishart, foreseeing his end, said, "Nay; return to thy pupils, and God bless you. One is sufficient for the sacrifice." And thus, while Wishart went to death, Knox was spared from death for great purposes. But Wishart greatly influenced him, for he left with him a book he had brought from the continent, Bullinger's Confession of Faith, the First Helvetic Confession.

The assassination of Cardinal Beaton, after Wishart's martyrdom, led to a reaction against the Protestants, from whose persecutions Knox only escaped by a constant change of residence. He finally, together with his pupils, took refuge (1547) in the castle of St. Andrew's, where the conspirators against Beaton were being besieged. In the chapel of the castle he resumed the instruction of his pupils on the Gospel of John. But this tutor of boys became the leader of men. Soon the garrison and the refugees gathered with them to hear his teaching. His ability and success led to his call into the ministry. John Rough, one of the ministers, preached one day on the ministry; and then, in the name of all present in the congregation, he made a public appeal to Knox to become a minister. Knox burst into tears and withdrew to his chamber, for he had scruples about accepting the responsibilities of so high an office. But the next Sunday he preached his first sermon against the papacy with such great force that his hearers said of him, "Maister Wishart spoke never so, and yet he was burned, even so will he be." Then in a disputation with the Catholics he, by the use of Scripture proofs, drove his opponents into a corner, so that the latter declared that when the apostles wrote their Epistles they had not yet received the Holy Ghost. He also celebrated the Lord's Supper like the Reformed on the continent.

IX. *Knox in the Galleys.*

After Knox had been at St. Andrew's about four months,

a French fleet appeared before the town and compelled it to surrender. The French took Knox with others as prisoners, and made them galley-slaves for nineteen months. Many years later he thus refers to his sufferings, "How long I continued in prison, and what torment I sustained in the galleys, and what were the sobs of my heart, there is no time to repeat." Other Reformers there were who died for their faith, but he then suffered a living death; and he was the only one of the Reformers who went through that sort of martyrdom.

Of this period two interesting incidents have come down to us. Soon after his galley arrived at Nantes, in France, a gaudily painted image of Mary was offered to one of them, probably Knox. He replied, "Trouble me not; such an object is accursed, and therefore I dare not touch it." But they forced it on him and put it between his hands. Whereat he threw it into the river, saying, "Let the lady now save herself. She is light enough. Let her learn to swim." The other incident occurred when his galley had been taken back to Scotland. As it lay opposite St. Andrew's, Knox, then very sick, was asked if he recognized St. Andrew's. "Yes," he replied, "I know it well, for I see the steeple of the place where I first opened my mouth to His glory." And then he added this prophecy, "And I am fully persuaded, though I am very sick now, that I shall not depart this life until my tongue shall glorify His godly name in the same place." This prophecy was, as we shall see, fulfilled many years after. At last, in 1549, he was set free.

X. *Knox in England.*

As a return to Scotland would mean that he would suffer the same fate as his spiritual father, Wishart, he remained in England, where Evangelical preachers were greatly needed since Edward VI had come to the throne. The Anglican Church licensed him, asking no questions as to whether he had been episcopally ordained. For five years, with true missionary zeal, he was a minister of that Church, first at Berwick and then at Newcastle on Tyne. Then he was appointed one of the royal chaplains, and often preached in London. He refused, it is said, the bishopric of Rochester. He left, however, a permanent impress on the Anglican Church by his opposition to kneeling at the Lord's Supper. This is shown in the Prayer-book of 1552, where a rubric was inserted explaining that this kneeling means no adoration of the elements. "This," said a later ritualist, "was the act of runagate Scot." But when Mary came to the throne of England he was compelled to flee, and went to the continent for four and a half years.

XI. *Knox on the Continent.*

In 1554 he was called to be pastor of the English Refugee Church at Frankfort, in Germany. And here during his pastorate occurred a great controversy which was the prophecy of the later Puritan controversy that so long divided the Anglican Church. His congregation was required by the Lutheran authorities of Frankfort to conform to the Calvinistic liturgy of the Walloon refugee church, which had come to Frankfort some time before them. So the Anglican Prayer-book was modified by leaving out the litany and the responses, together with a few other changes. These changes suited Knox and some of the congregation who preferred the simpler Reformed worship. But later a colony of English refugees arrived, led by Cox, who had been one of the compilers of the Prayer-book. They demanded the full use of that liturgy. And, by bringing a charge of treason against Knox for having compared the Emperor Charles V to Nero, they led the city government to demand Knox's departure. He went to Geneva, where he was gladly welcomed by Calvin, who had sympathized with him in his troubles at Frankford, and had written him a letter in which he speaks of the Anglican Prayer-book as having "many tolerably foolish things,"— a charge for which the Anglican Church has never forgiven him. Knox organized the English Church at Geneva, and soon the congregation numbered more than two hundred. His stay at Geneva was the happiest time of his life. There he had the kind of worship he liked, and also a congenial friend in Calvin, to whom he always looked up as a father. And his congregation, too, had in it scholars of first rank, as Coverdale. The congregation, though small, was charged with great destinies, for out of it came Presbyterianism in Scotland and also Puritanism in England. One of its most influential acts was the publication by Whittingham of the Genevan Bible, the most popular of the early English versions.

XII. *Knox's Return to Scotland.*

After twelve years of exile from Scotland, during which time he had visited his native land once (1555-6), he started to return to Scotland after the death of Queen Mary of England in 1558. He was, however, halted at Dieppe by his friends in Scotland, countermanding their invitation to him to return. So, as he was possessed of the true missionary spirit, he began preaching for the Huguenots at Dieppe. He founded the Huguenot Church there, and his converts were so many that it afterward became one of the strongholds of the Reformed Church of France.

Finally the way opened for him to return to Scotland, May 2, 1559. The Reformation had been gaining power there, especially among the nobles, so that in December, 1557, the Protestant nobles had drawn up a covenant, which organized them into a party. The political situation helped their cause, as many of the Scotch had grown restive against the growing domination of France in Scotch affairs. Knox arrived at Scotland at the psychological moment. Although much of the political power of the Protestants had been due to James Stewart and the Duke of Argyle, yet it was due no less to Knox, for in him Protestantism found a religious leader. He became the great missionary and evangelist to call Scotland to Christ. The crisis that occurred when he arrived was that the Queen Regent had ordered the Protestant preachers to appear before her at Stirling, May 10, 1559. Instead they gathered at Perth, and there Knox made his first public appearance in Scotland with the Dundee contingent. There Knox sounded the trumpet call of Protestantism by preaching a series of sermons against the idolatries of Rome. At the end of one of his sermons a priest came in to celebrate mass. As a boy made some comment on his act, the priest gave him a cuff on the ear. But the boy was ready, and retaliated with a stone, which, missing the priest, struck and broke an image. That was a sufficient signal. The Protestants cleared the churches of images and relics of Romanism. The Regent saw in this an opportunity against Protestantism, so she marched her army against Perth. It finally surrendered. But she violated her promise to them to permit Protestant worship.

So the Protestants withdrew to St. Andrew's. And so Knox fulfilled his prophecy of years before,—he preached the Gospel again at St. Andrew's. Then the Protestants captured Perth and Edinburgh, and Knox preached there in St. Giles Cathedral. Then the tide turned, for the Catholics received help from France. The Protestants were defeated at Leith, and retreated in great disorder to Stirling and St. Andrew's. Knox went to the latter place. The Regent tried to drive them out of St. Andrew's. Their extremity was then so great that the Regent exclaimed, "Where is now John Knox, his God? My God is stronger than his, yes, even in Fife."* Knox's anxiety now pierced his heart more than all the torments of the galleys. But still he never doubted that the Gospel would triumph. Then providence sent help. England sent an army, so that they captured Edinburgh. By July 6 peace was made, and the Protestants were masters of the kingdom. Knox in all

* The district of Fife was largely Protestant.

these campaigns was not only army-chaplain, but he was also secretary, penning dispatches and negotiating with England for help, yes, even haggling with her about the sums of money to be paid to the Scotch nobles, it was said. But his voice put more fire into the men than five hundred trumpets.

However, though peace had come, much still remained to be done. The appeal that had most influenced Scotland had been political and not religious. The nobles had grown jealous of the foreign French dominion. It remained for Knox to complete this political reformation by a religious reformation. Fortunately the state was now on his side, and one of the early acts of the Scotch Parliament of 1560 was the forbidding of the mass, under severe penalties.

XIII. *Knox and Mary, Queen of Scots.*

Suddenly an event occurred that changed the whole situation. Queen Mary returned from France to Scotland on August 19, 1561. Then came the tremendous struggle between Knox and Queen Mary—one of the great duels in history between two religions and also between fashion and worldliness in Mary on the one side, and intense spirituality and Puritanism in Knox on the other. On the Sunday after her arrival, she celebrated mass in Holyrood Castle, just south of Edinburgh. Knox thundered against this from his pulpit at St. Giles Cathedral in Edinburgh, about a mile away. He declared that the mass was forbidden by law, and said that "one mass was more fearful to him than the landing of ten thousand armed enemies." Mary decided to win him, and so invited him to an interview in her castle, August 26. But she found a man on whom her smiles and blandishments, usually so powerful, had no effect. His replies completely silenced her. A second time he was called before her, for a sermon that he had preached against the persecutions of the Huguenots in France, in celebration of which the queen had had a ball at Holyrood castle. As he was going out of this interview, some papists, seeing his "merry countenance," said of him, "He is not afraid." He overheard it, and replied, "Why should the pleasing face of a gentlewoman make me afraid? I have looked into the faces of many angry men, and yet not been afraid above measure." But the most stormy interview occurred in June, 1563, when the rumor went abroad that Mary was to marry the Catholic king of Spain. Knox denounced this with such force from his pulpit that even his friends were displeased. The queen, when he came in, was in a towering passion, and she had called him to the castle for the express purpose of silencing him. But Knox was not a man to be silenced, especially when he believed religion to be at stake. During the period of these interviews, of which there were five, Knox was virtually the uncrowned king of Scotland, as at St. Giles Cathedral he thundered against Mary and the papacy in Holyrood palace.

But after this last interview Knox's life was in peril, for the queen's example was telling on the country. Those who came up to Edinburgh to protest against her celebration of the mass somehow cooled when they came into contact with her court. And they went home with the idea that the mass was not so dangerous after all. The holy water of the court sprinkled on them took away their fervency. The priests took advantage of this feeling, and here and there throughout the land they began to celebrate mass. It was a question whether the queen might not ultimately gain the day, especially as Mary's blandishments were undermining the virtue of the Protestant nobility.

But suddenly Mary threw all her chances away. She married her cousin, Darnley. This act cost her some of her best counsellors. Darnley, though young and beautiful, was a fool, and she soon tired of him for Rizzio, an Italian of her court. Then Rizzio, her favorite, was assassinated, March 9, 1566. Matters, however, had been dark for the Protestants after the queen's marriage, especially as Knox had been forbidden to preach in Edinburg when the king and queen were there. They became darker after the assassination of Rizzio, for some of the Protestant leaders were implicated in that act and had to flee. Knox had to retire to Ayrshire. He returned, however, to Edinburgh, as Mary's new favorite was the Earl of Bothwell, a nominal Protestant. But just then the queen restored the Catholic archbishop of St. Andrew's to his jurisdiction. This was the most daring act that Mary had done, and Knox knew not what to expect next. Then Darnley was assassinated. And three months after, the queen was married to Bothwell. Horror at this caused a revolution against Mary on the part of many of the Scotch nobles, both Catholic and Protestant. Mary's forces were defeated, and she was imprisoned in Loch Leven Castle. Mary's infant son, James, was crowned king, and Knox preached the coronation sermon on the Coronation of Joash. The next parliament in 1567 confirmed the acts of 1560, forbidding Catholicism in Scotland. On May 2, 1568, Mary escaped from Loch Leven and took refuge in England. Thus Knox and Protestantism triumphed.

XIV. *Knox's Last Years.*

But, alas, the good Protestant regent, Moray, was soon after assassinated, January 23, 1570, an irreparable loss to Knox. The situation was still somewhat uncertain in Scotland. Even the castle at Edinburgh sided with Mary against the Protestants who controlled the city. Knox was in danger. A shot was fired into his house, but missed him because he accidentally, or, rather, providentially, had left his accustomed seat. By this time Knox began to reveal the infirmities of age, superinduced by his worries and cares. He was now a broken man physically. His last public act was the installation of his successor, Lawson, at St. Giles Cathedral. His voice was then so weak that he could not be heard in that great edifice. The last night of his life he had a great wrestling with a new temptation, namely, that his good works were sufficient in the sight of God to save him. Later asked to give a parting sign that he was in peace, he lifted his hand and passed away. At his funeral the regent, Morton, uttered the memorable eulogy, "Here lies one who neither flattered nor feared any flesh."

XV. *His Character.*

So died Knox, a man of superb *faith* in the face of greatest difficulties,—a man of *impulsiveness*, so that he sometimes made mistakes. But he was a man of *prayer*, so that Queen Mary trembled at his prayers. He more nearly approached Farel in his character than any of the other Reformers, except that he had certain elements of Calvin's statesmanship. He had the fervor peculiar to the Scotch in oratory. When he preached, he fused logic and passion, and stormed at once the head and the heart of his hearers. Says his biographer, "He was one of the four great Scotchmen," Buchanan, Burns and Carlyle being the other three.

XVI. *Conclusion.*

In closing this work, the author can only express the hope that this study of the zeal of the Reformers for the salvation of their age may prove to be a stimulus to us to be missionaries in our age. How much we owe to the Reformers of the sixteenth century! But for them we would still be in the superstitions and darkness of Romanism. Shall we not show our thankfulness to them by giving the precious Gospel of God's grace, which they preached, to those in our day who have it not? May their missionary zeal lay hold of us, and may the Spirit of God so fill all who study this book that we may have a new era of the Evangelism of the Reformation.

www.ingramcontent.com/pod-product-compliance
Lightning Source LLC
Chambersburg PA
CBHW032116090426
42743CB00007B/367